*Resurrection*

# RESURRECTION

Biblical Testimony to the Resurrection:
An Historical Examination and Explanation

## ULRICH WILCKENS

Translated by A. M. Stewart

**JOHN KNOX PRESS**
ATLANTA

This edition published in 1978 by
JOHN KNOX PRESS, Atlanta

Published in Great Britain by The Saint Andrew Press
English translation © 1977 The Saint Andrew Press

This book was first published in German by
Kreuz-Verlag Erich Breitsohl und Co. KG,
D 7000, Stuttgart 80, under the title
'Auferstehung' (Themen der Theologie, Band 4).
© 1970 Kreuz-Verlag Stuttgart


**Library of Congress Cataloging in Publication Data**

Wilckens, Ulrich, 1928-
    Resurrection.

    Translation of Auferstehung.
    Includes bibliographical references.
    1. Resurrection—Biblical teaching.
2. Jesus Christ—Resurrection.   I. Title.
BS680.R37W513   1978      236′.8      77-15752
ISBN 0-8042-0396-2




ISBN 0-8042-0396-2
Printed in the United States of America

# Contents

# Preface

For those readers who are of the firm opinion that acceptance of the Biblical testimony of the resurrection of Jesus just simply can no longer be expected of a modern person, and for those readers who consider it a sacrilege to expose to scientific examination the testimony of faith in Biblical revelation, this book is presumably unlikely to be helpful or even convincing reading. For, on the one hand, an attempt is made to make the Biblical testimony to the resurrection clear and comprehensible in its original significance, in accordance with all the rules of rational and historical methods, without allowing ourselves to be misled by prejudices of belief or unbelief. On the other hand, the author allows himself to be guided by the conviction that what was once of central significance for Christians and has proven itself to be of central importance through so many centuries of Christian history, is unlikely to have become, all-of-a-sudden, meaningless for us as Christians today.

The author shares neither the delight (which has once again become fashionable nowadays) in the destruction of tradition which has survived, for the sake of something completely new; nor the diehard spirit of those who seek to seal-off the fortress of tradition from all that is modern. For those readers, however, who are anxious to find out as precisely and thoroughly as possible what the earliest Christians really meant when they spoke of the resurrection of Jesus, this book is intended as a reliable aid.

The book does not set out to prescribe or suggest what the reader has to think about the testimony to the resurrection in the New Testament. The decision about that is left to the reader himself, and the author concentrates instead on providing detailed information permitting a solidly-based judgment to be formed.

It was necessary, for considerations of space within the scope of this series, to omit an introduction to the history and present state of research, and a reasoned discussion of the varying and sometimes contradictory opinions and judgments of other scholars in the field. Almost every sentence will reveal to the knowledgeable reader the author's agreement or disagreement with all the important theses put forward in older and more recent writing.

The non-specialist can rest assured that nothing important in relevant research is being withheld. I am further obliged to give due recognition and special mention to the unpublished work of Dr Klaus Berger and Eckhard Rau. I am indebted to both of them for vital insights into Jewish expectation of resurrection: to the first-mentioned for what is said about expectation of Elijah and to the latter for the interpretation of Enoch 22. Scholarly work flourishes best in collaboration. This is the appropriate place to thank both of these colleagues most heartily for their enrichment of my experience.

ULRICH WILCKENS

## NOTE

Abbreviations used:

RSV      = Revised Standard Version
NEB      = New English Bible
Charles = *The Apocrypha and Pseudepigrapha of The Old Testament in English*, edited by R. H. Charles (2 vols, Oxford, 1913, reissued 1963)

New Testament quotations are from NEB to conform to the style of the German original.

# Chapter One

# Resurrection in the New Testament

The reader wishing to make a scholarly investigation of the Biblical testimony to the resurrection must first of all find out about the sources and carefully compare their statements in order to arrange them in their proper place within the history of primitive Christianity. For it is only when we know when and where, in which milieu and in which situation, the various authors made these statements, that we are able to give proper weight to their testimony, understand its original meaning, and evaluate its significance.

## 1. THE SOURCES AND THEIR HISTORY

As one might expect, there are no non-Christian witnesses of any sort who could give us information about the resurrection of Jesus and his appearances, or comment from a non-Christian aspect on the statements made about the resurrection by the early Christians, important as such comments would be for a historically accurate picture.

Already the first anti-Christian polemicist of any stature, the Greek philosopher Celsus (AD 178), speaks mockingly of the fact that Jesus, if he actually arose again, did not appear to his opponents nor to the judge who condemned him, nor indeed to everybody, but only to his own supporters and followers. Any Jewish polemics we have are of much later origin. For the first century we are, without exception, forced to rely on the testimony of the Christians. Therefore we must expect that all testimonies are determined by their faith, its viewpoint and its interests. There are no such things as 'pure factual accounts'. The earliest Christians are undoubtedly the last people from whom such purely factual accounts were to be expected. The

1

writings which have to be taken into account can be fairly
unambiguously dated. The oldest documents of the New
Testament are Paul's Letters. The First Letter to the
Corinthians, in Chapter 15 of which there is a summary of all
the Easter traditions known to Paul, dates from AD 54 or 55.
The Gospels were all written later. According to the almost
unanimous agreement of researchers the oldest of the Gospels
is that according to St Mark, written shortly before or after
AD 70. Independently of each other, the writers of the Gospels
of St Matthew and St Luke, based their accounts on it. These
two Gospels are therefore usually dated towards the end of the
first century.

St John's Gospel dates from approximately the same time.
It shows in its Easter account a certain proximity to St Luke's
Gospel. However it can probably not be assumed that the
writer of the former used the latter. Both evangelists seem to
have had some similar narrative context from oral tradition.
Finally, from a later period, there are a number of Gospel
writings which have not been accepted in the canon of the New
Testament. Of these, St Peter's Gospel is of interest to us. At
the end, it has an Easter story which strongly impinges on the
account in Matthew, but has clearly decorated the account
with naive-phantastic dramatic effect.

Yet the dates of composition of the individual writings cannot
serve as a criterion for a verdict about the age of the contents
related in them. Research of the last decades has learned
indeed to distinguish in these writings materials which the
authors knew from communal oral tradition and processed in
their works. This is applicable, for example, to the short
summary of the Easter events in 1 Corinthians 15. Paul says
there, expressly, that he himself had already 'received' the
account, and what he had 'taken over' he had then 'handed
over' to the community at its foundation. That is to say, the
material collected here indubitably goes back to the oldest
phase of all in the history of primitive Christianity.

Also, the materials of the Easter accounts in the Gospels had all already gone through a historical process of oral tradition within the community before they were creatively structured in writing by the Gospel writers. It is therefore possible, from the point of view of *method*, that some parts in writings which are, in *literary* terms, of a later date, are nevertheless, in terms of their place in *tradition*, of great antiquity. For example, the later date of St Mark's Gospel compared with First Corinthians does not necessarily imply that Mark's account was compiled after Paul.

When Paul in his letters at no point unambiguously indicates his knowledge of the story of Jesus's empty tomb, this fact alone does not justify the conclusion that we must therefore be dealing with a narrative first recounted after the time of Paul. If it were a post-Pauline account that would of course be relevant to its evaluation in historical terms. Recognition of the fact that there was a period of broad oral tradition with many layers to it, intervening before our written documents came into existence, does not make it in any way easier for researchers to form a valid judgment: on the contrary it makes it much more complicated. At the same time, however, recognition of this fact has considerably improved the possibility of gaining insights into the earliest periods of primitive Christian tradition. A consequence of this for research methods is that we have to compare carefully individual items of information and narrative with each other; and simultaneously consider not only their literary age but also their location in the history of oral tradition.

However, that is not all. At the same time we must always seek an explanation for the appearance of these materials in the tradition of the community. For, if the writers were not the first to form these strands, then different grounds than those usually applied to literary products in general must be found in order to account for their appearance. They are neither products of creative writing or poetic art, nor are they, for example, historiographical works. They cannot be explained in terms of any literary intention of an author, but on the contrary only in terms of the social needs of the life of those communities in which the materials were created and for whose use they were intended. Therefore investigation must be made into the conditions of Christian community life in primitive Christianity, under which the need arose to transmit such traditional material.

The method of investigating texts analysing the history of the form has been developed since the 1920s and nowadays is part of the essential arsenal of methods not only of Biblical exegesis but also of all literary studies dealing with popular composition and oral transmission. As far as the primitive Christian Easter testimonies are concerned, we cannot start off with any detailed analyses of form. Nevertheless attention must be drawn to one point of view which will be important for the following studies, namely, that apparently tradition was transmitted in various differing situations, and that, accordingly, this led to various differing forms of tradition. This is true of all New Testament material, and likewise for the Easter accounts: they are not to be dealt with all on one and the same level. The missionaries, for example, spoke differently about Jesus rising from the dead, than did those speaking within the context of the divine service of the Christian communities. Even within the divine service too, however, the message of his rising from the dead sounded differently in the Hymns in Praise of the Risen Lord and in the account read out aloud narrating the story of his Passion.

The short catalogue-like summary of the various appearances of the risen Lord in First Corinthians 15:5–7 must have served other purposes than the extended story, structured with narrative skill and artistry, recounting the encounter of the two disciples with their master whom they did not recognize, in Luke 24:13ff. The former is evidently formulated for learning by heart; the latter is designed to hold the admiring wonder of an audience. Thus the former indicates its catechetical use, and indeed it was virtually termed a small catechism. The latter could represent the reading in divine service, in a community holding fast to the narration of the history of its own origins.

Finally it will be necessary to take into consideration that the communities in primitive Christianity were by no means all identical, and so have not all handed down the same materials in their traditions. Whereas, for example, Paul as missionary proclaimed at the centre of his preaching the death and resurrection of Christ, the similar collections of sayings in Luke 10 and Matthew 10 give precedence to a group of disciples who in accordance with Jesus's directions proclaimed the imminence of the Kingdom of God (Matt. 10:7) as Jesus himself had done (Matt. 4:12ff). Of Christ's resurrection no mention is made; it is admittedly doubtless taken for granted, but it is not, as in the case of Paul, the central content of missionary preaching.

In Paul's writings, on the other hand, the central keyword of Jesus's sermon, namely the Kingdom of God, is only peripheral, in the moral instruction, not in the preaching of mission (cf. e.g. 1 Cor. 6:9f; Gal. 5:21; Romans 14:17); and, whereas in Paul's writings and in 1 Peter and the Letter to the Hebrews there is mention of the resurrection in contemplating the risen Lord in Heaven; and, whereas the laudatory statements, about his elevation and his heavenly position of power and his function as Lord, immediately follow on from the preaching of his resurrection; according to the Gospel of St Luke and the Acts of the Apostles, the main point is to see the resurrection of Jesus as an event happening within the framework of his earthly story (cf. e.g. Acts 10:37–42).

These are all differences in the overall picture which must not be harmonized, but distinguished as probably being explicable by assuming that different communities transmitted different aspects of the tradition. Thus it becomes clear, that, just as the New Testament writings come from different times and situations, so too the various orally-formed traditions which the New Testament writings incorporate also come from different areas of the life of the early Christians and from various different communities.

The analysis of texts on the basis of the history of forms yields quite surprising insights beyond the most ancient writings, into the preceding earliest phase of the history of the traditions of primitive Christianity—before Mark and before Paul. On the other hand too, equally, it emphasizes the fact that precisely in the earliest period the Church had by no means a self-contained, rounded off, unified tradition; on the contrary it displayed major variations from place to place. It is advisable therefore to consider the various different testimonies, first of all, within their own sphere of tradition; and only to assume and evaluate connections between them where these links are clearly shown.

## 2. THE PROCLAMATION OF THE RESURRECTION IN THE LETTERS OF PAUL

In the letters of Paul there are some passages where one can more or less unambiguously discern how the earliest mission communities in primitive Christianity spoke about the resurrection of Jesus. These passages demand to be given priority, for after all we are seeking primarily to gain an insight into the earliest phase of Christian belief in the resurrection.

### (a)  *1 Corinthians 15 : 3–7*

One such passage demanding priority of our attention is certainly the short catechism-like fragment of tradition contained in 1 Cor. 15:3–5. Paul stresses that he himself is taking it over as an established tradition (v.1f) and all other missionaries proclaimed the same (v.11). Thus it is on the one hand very old, and on the other hand very widespread. We must therefore consider this passage first of all. Furthermore, the sentences in verses 3 to 5 stand out in relief from the context by their artistic arrangement and precise and stringent formulation:

> I. 'Christ died for our sins, in accordance with the scriptures.
> II. He was buried.
> III. He was raised to life on the third day, according to the scriptures.

IV. He appeared to Cephas, and afterwards to the Twelve.'
(NEB)

The centre is formed by the two sentences about the death and resurrection of Christ (I and III). They correspond in their tripartite affirmation and in their concurring references to the 'scriptures'. The shorter sentences II and IV are attached to them respectively. Burial reinforces the death, the appearances underline and emphasize the resurrection. The whole piece is held together by the one subject which dominates the beginning—'Christ'.

This name is the Greek rendering of the Hebrew 'maschiach' (Messiah) = 'the anointed', with which surrounding Jewish people designated the King of David's race, whose imminent appearance was awaited with longing as the Saviour sent by God. The Christians believed that the Messiah had come in Jesus, however, not as a victorious military leader against Israel's foes, but as the Crucified One who had died to atone for our sins and who had been raised by God from the dead. Thus the Jewish name of Messiah had assumed a very special sense in the language of the earliest Christians right from the beginning. As such this name was also used so much as a matter of course that one can often be in some doubt as to what extent 'Christ' is still to be regarded as a title of Messiah and to what extent it is already simply a proper name of the crucified one, a name whose sense was totally determined by the significance of his death and his resurrection. In Mark's account of his Passion this Christian redefinition or re-minting of the Jewish Messiah title strikes the eye at one particular point. Over the crucified Lord a notice was placed, with an inscription giving the charge against him reading 'The King of the Jews' (Mark 15:26). The old article of faith in 1 Cor. 15:3 says something similar when it emphatically places 'Christ' at the beginning. The Messiah sent by God—is this One—is the Crucified One.

The first sentence, about the effect of Christ's death bringing salvation, cannot be expounded within the restricted limits of this volume. The weight ascribed to this sentence in the series of affirmations can be gauged by the fact that only in this first sentence is there reference to the significance to us for our salvation 'Christ died for our sins'. The tradition with regard to the Lord's Supper makes a corresponding statement. In St Paul's version (1 Cor. 11:24), referring to the bread, it says 'This is my body, which is (given into death) for you'. In St Mark's Gospel it is said of the cup: 'This is my blood, through which the covenant is strengthened, shed for many' (Mark 14:24).

The Last Supper is reported in the framework of the story of the Passion, and Paul, too, implies that he knows the introductory words in the context of a report of the events 'on the night on which he was handed over' (1 Cor. 11:23). Now, since in the 'Formula' (1 Cor. 15:3–5) the sentence about Jesus's death for our sins is followed by details of his burial and resurrection, and since these correspond to both the concluding scenes of St Mark's story of the Passion (Mark 15:42; 16:1ff), then it is reasonable to suppose that correspondingly the statement about the atoning death of Christ (v.3) refers to the scene of the Last Supper in the narrative context of the account of the Passion. The formulation as a whole would then prove to be a condensed summary of the story of the Passion of Jesus.

That the short sentence about the burial of Jesus (II) pre-supposes the corresponding Gospel narrative, cannot be stringently proven, but it is the most probable assumption to make. For the interpretation that the mention of burial is only in order to underline the reality of death so that death and burial belong together in the closest way (cf. Acts 2:29; Luke 16:22; Isa. 53:9) is excluded by the fact that the sentence in the series of formulaic statements, despite its brevity, has the same independence and weight as the other three sentences.

There is thus a separate interest of its own in the record of the fact of the burial. That can be explained by the fact that in Judaism one did not speak only of the burial of the dead, if one were speaking of their death, but one also looked after and honoured and respected the burial places themselves (cf. Acts 2:29; Matt. 23:29). Precisely this intention is undoubtedly behind the account of the burial within the framework of the story of the Passion. That the narrative betrays definite knowledge of the location is therefore very likely; indeed many biblical interpreters even suspect that it is a question of a cultic report in the framework of a divine service celebrated by the Jerusalem community at the tomb of Jesus. To this the objection has often been made that Paul nowhere else in his letters shows a knowledge of the story of the burial. That is correct. Yet that need not contradict the conjecture we have expressed. For, outside Jerusalem, in the mission communities of Asia Minor and Greece, the concrete meaning which the narrative had for the Christians in Jerusalem can understandably have paled into insignificance and contracted until it is a mere *item of data* in the tradition of the faith.

After all, nowhere else either in the Letters of Paul is there revealed any knowledge of details of the events of the Passion, yet it can be inferred from the formulation of the tradition concerning the Lord's Supper in 1 Cor. 11:23, that Paul was aware of its connection with it. As the Passion story, at least originally, was the framework of the opening words of the institution, so too correspondingly the tradition handed down in 1 Cor. 15:3f, when it was written down, can have taken its orientation from an old form of the account of the Passion. Incidentally, 1 Cor. 15:4 is not the only passage containing a mention of the burial of Jesus. At Colossians 2:12 baptism is described as participation in Christ's death, burial and resurrection, and at Romans 6:3f Paul interprets the thought, which it is taken for granted will be familiar to the readers, concerning the forgiveness of sins experienced in baptism, namely, that in the tomb into which the dead Jesus was laid, there lay with him also our sin, for Christ, after all, died 'for our sins', and just as he arose out of death and the tomb, so too through him we have become free from our sin, and have become able and duty-bound to do what is just and act in righteousness. The tomb of Christ has here, completely, become a point in theological argument. Nevertheless here we have the same succession of death, burial and resurrection as in 1 Cor. 15:4. So the conjecture cannot be rejected that the statement about the resurrection in 1 Cor. 15:4 (III) originally took its orientation from the Easter story, with which the account of the Passion concludes, namely the story of the empty grave in Mark 16:1–8. This verdict is admittedly a matter of great controversy among researchers. In so far as the contradictory verdicts about the age of this story affect this, we are not yet in any position to adopt a definitive stance in this investigation.

On the contrary, as far as the passage in Paul is concerned, it must first of all be admitted, as in the case of the statement about the burial, that the apostle nowhere in his letters reveals any knowledge of the contents of Mark 16:1–8. But this can have the same grounds as in the former case, and accordingly does not mean we must necessarily come to a negative verdict. What does support the conjecture expressed above is the fact that we are told that Christ arose from the dead 'on the third day'. This fact exactly corresponds to the narrative sequence in Mark 16 where it is the early morning of the first day of the week, the third day after Jesus's death, on which the women find Jesus's tomb opened and the angel in the sepulchre reveals to them the message of his resurrection. The 'third day' became a fixed formulation in primitive Christian tradition (cf. Acts 10:40) and it also emerges again later in the second article of the Roman confession of faith in this form. Apart from the reference to Mark 16 the sense of this formulation can not be found, and without it we have no convincing explanation how it arose.

Since, according to 1 Cor. 15:4 the resurrection took place on the third day 'according to the scriptures', it has been conjectured alternatively that an Old Testament passage (Hosea 6:11f), which compares God's help to the people of Israel with resurrection from the dead 'on the third day', stimulated the formulation of the primitive Christian statement about the resurrection. But neither does 1 Cor. 15:3f refer to any specific passages of scripture—the passage indeed concerns the general basic verdict that the whole of the Passion and Easter story of Jesus have taken place in fulfilment of the will of God, and, therefore, 'according to the scriptures' (cf. Luke 24:26f, 44f; Acts 17:2f, 11; Romans 1:2; 1 Peter 1:10f)—nor indeed, above all, is there, in all the writings of primitive Christianity, one single passage where reference is made to Hosea 6.

There is also a passage in Matt. 12:40 which is brought in to explain the 'third day'. Here the resurrection of Jesus is compared with the fate of the prophet Jonah, who had to spend 'three days and three nights' in the belly of the giant fish (Jon. 2:1). Yet this passage demonstrably is a late subsequent attempt to explain an old puzzling saying of Jesus, which is given in its original form in Luke (Luke 11:29); secondly, however, it is not a question here of the resurrection 'on the third day', but 'after three days and three nights'. It is difficult to explain how the former could arise from the latter, whereas the reverse process is easily understandable: namely, the similar sound of the fixed formula of 'the third day' led to a similar sounding time-reference in the Book of Jonah being taken, after the event, as being a prediction of Jesus's resurrection. Derivation from the Old Testament is thus very improbable. Unless one wishes to explain it in more general terms as a product of the effect, on the testimony concerning the resurrection in primitive Christianity, of the widespread popular belief of the time, according to which the soul of a deceased person remained for a short period of about three days in the proximity of the body before leaving it entirely, then preference must be given to the explanation suggested above: namely, that the pre-Pauline formulation of belief found in 1 Cor. 15:3f, was, in its statements about the death, burial and resurrection of Christ on the third day, guided by the narrative context of the Passion and Easter story as attested in the Gospel according to St Mark.

Now, the statement about the resurrection is linked with a series of *appearances of the risen Lord* of which the first two (1 Cor. 15:5) undoubtedly belong to the formulation (IV) of the article of belief in verses 3 to 5. Here an appearance to Peter, who is here named by his Aramaic name of Cephas, is mentioned together with a subsequent appearance to the Twelve. There is a corresponding linking of an appearance to an individual and an appearance to a group in 1 Cor. 15:7: 'He appeared to James, then to all the apostles'. This striking resemblance in form between v.5 and v.7 has led to the supposition that 7 was later modelled on 5. In fact there is reflected in the sequence, Peter and the circle of the Twelve leading on to James and a larger circle of missionaries (apostles), the history of the conditions in the leadership of the Jerusalem Christian community. Initially the group of the Twelve of which Peter was the spokesman, formed the central leadership body (Acts 2–5). Soon, however, the family of Jesus, with James at the head, came from Galilee to the Jerusalem community of disciples of Jesus, and it was only too easy to understand that they were allotted a special position of honour. At the first visit which Paul, after his conversion, paid to Peter in Jerusalem, he already saw the brother of Jesus (Gal. 1:18f).

When fourteen years later Paul, together with Barnabas, went to the decisive negotiations between the Syrian Metropolis of the mission to the heathen in Antioch and the Jerusalem leaders, on his second visit to Jerusalem, James is already the leading spokesman. Peter and John, as representatives of the old leading circle of the Twelve, are ranked beside him (Gal. 2:1–10). Finally, in the subsequent period, Peter is seen as the missionary out in the mission communities, in compliance with the Jerusalem decision (Gal. 2:7f); whereas James is sole leader in Jerusalem surrounded by 'elders' (Acts 21:17ff).

The two corresponding formulations in 1 Cor. 15:5 and 7 thus do in fact reflect the history of the original Christian community, and that sheds light on the sense and function of these short sentences in their formulaic fixed form for handing down in tradition; namely, in naming the appearances of our risen Lord which were made to the Christians of the initial period, and by naming them by their names, there was expressed the authority which the latter had received in person by their encounter with the risen Lord himself. These are 'legitimation formulae', that is, the appearances are kept embodied in the tradition because they are seen as demonstrating that the leaders of primitive Christianity received their legitimation, their mandate, their vocation and calling, and their position of full power and authority, from Heaven. At any rate Paul himself regarded the appearance to him (1 Cor. 15:8) in this sense. Paul only mentions the appearance in his Letters where it concerns his calling to be an apostle (Gal. 1:15f; Rom. 1:1–5). 'Am I not an apostle? Have I not seen the Lord?' (1 Cor. 9:1). These questions belong together, and show especially clearly that the essential significance of the appearance of our risen Lord, as Paul understands it, has not so much to do with his conversion to belief in Christ, but rather it has to do with his calling to be an apostle.

What is valid as far as Paul is concerned, can also be assumed to apply to those who experienced an encounter with our risen Lord before Paul. That it is true at any rate for Peter seems to be shown by a few really clear indications in tradition. In the next section we shall argue that the angel's prophecy at the empty tomb (at Mark 16:7) foretelling Jesus's appearance to his 'disciples and to Peter' is to be understood in the sense of their being called to proclaim and preach the Gospel. And the late account of the Galilean appearance (John 21) has its objective in the thrice-repeated injunction to Peter to feed Jesus's sheep (vv. 15, 16, 17). The purpose is surely similar too in the word to Peter at Luke 22:32, that after his conversion he ought to strengthen his brethren.

But above all, the famous saying (Matt. 16:18) adjudges Peter to be the rock on which Jesus wants to erect the eternal edifice of his Church, and gives Peter charge of the keys of the Heavenly Kingdom. Many Biblical interpreters, with justification, regard this as incorporating what seems to have been originally a saying of the risen Lord in which the significance of the first appearance to the leader of the Twelve as being the 'man of rock' was especially clearly expressed. Also, as far as the appearance to the Twelve is concerned, the old tradition points in the same direction. According to Matthew, Luke and John, Jesus appears to them in order to send them out as messengers: one saying from ancient tradition places them as rulers over the Twelve tribes of the community of Israel attaining salvation at the end of time (Matt. 19:28; cf. Luke 22:28–30); but according to the prophecy in Revelation (21:14) they will be the twelve foundations on which the Holy City of the Last Days will be built (cf. Matt. 16:18). It is a riddle how here talk is everywhere of the Twelve, whereas according to the Gospel tradition which has previously reported about the betrayal by Judas, Jesus only appears to the Eleven.

The Acts of the Apostles solves the riddle, when it reports about a second or by-election to bring the number up to twelve again (Acts 1:15–26). That is certainly not, as some suggest, an invention by Luke, but on the contrary already passed on to him as tradition; but whether it is old and accurate must be seriously questioned in view of the contradictory item of information in 1 Cor. 15:5 which certainly goes back to the most ancient tradition. So it is easier to accept the assumption that the number Twelve had already become a fixed concept because of the work of the group prior to the Easter event, with the result that people referred to the appearance to the Twelve although in reality only eleven were present, and later tradition then corrected this.

In any case the Twelve are not identical with the circle of 'all the apostles' (1 Cor. 15:7). This undoubtedly refers to a considerably larger number, to which there belonged also, we can assume, some of the first Antioch missionaries, for example Barnabas, mentioned at 1 Cor. 9:6, and the two apostles Andronicus and Junias, mentioned in Rom. 16:7.

The name apostle (messenger, envoy, of Jesus) tells us that his appearance to them, which they relate, likewise was taken by them as applying to their call to vocation, their assignment to their divine mission. There only remains to be discussed the appearance recorded in 1 Cor. 15:6—'Then he appeared to over five hundred of our brothers at once, most of whom are still alive, though some have died' (NEB). That Paul here—in contrast to the two sentences 1 Cor. 15:5 and 15:7—is not quoting some fixed formulation, but on the contrary some less rigidly transmitted item of information, is already shown by the differing style of the sentence. Paul refers to the fact that the Christians participating in the experience of this manifestation are known and can be questioned at any time as witnesses. What we are concerned with here is thus a definite larger circle of Christians expressly singled out. Some Biblical interpreters have suspected that an early form of the Whitsun story in Acts 2 might be the basis here. But there it is not a question of the appearance of the risen Lord, but of a wonderful inspiration through the Spirit of God.

Therefore it is more likely to refer to supporters of Jesus who have come together in view of his appearances to Peter and the Twelve, in order to form a community of disciples of Jesus after the Easter events, and who now themselves are all collectively validated, by an appearance of his, as God's community for salvation at the Day of Judgment. These community members of the beginning then held a prominent specially-singled-out position of honour within the Jerusalem primitive Christian community—so Paul can assume that they were all individually known.

Let us summarize the results of our examination of 1 Cor. 15:3–7.

1. Paul quotes in vv. 3–5 a catechism-like piece of tradition, quoting verbally a version reaching back to the earliest period in the history of Christianity.
2. The individual statements contained in this 'catechism' seem to take their guidance from an old account of the

Passion, in which the report of the Last Supper, the burial
and the events of Easter are stressed in their basic
significance within the framework of the proclamation
and preaching of salvation.

3. Mention of the appearances to Peter and the Twelve is
not taken (as still has to be shown) from the narrative
context of the Passion story, but developed out of a
separate tradition. Here it is a matter of demonstrating
the authority of certain leaders, specifically named,
showing their authority to have been conferred on them
by an appearance to them of the risen Lord, and it is a
matter of establishing this in the tradition in 'legitimation
formulae'.

Mention of the appearance of Jesus to his brother
James and to the circle of 'all apostles' (1 Cor. 15:7) is of
the same kind. Only the appearance to 'over five hundred
brothers' (1 Cor. 15:6) appears not to be transmitted in a
formulaic fixed form; Paul here appears to be alluding to
a Jerusalem narrative.

(b) *The Conceptual Context of the Proclamation of the Resurrection*

Now that the examination of 1 Cor. 15:3–7 has given an
insight into the traditional context of the early Easter
testimonies, the next step has to be taken with the question:
How did Paul really understand the resurrection of Jesus?
What concept or connotations did he link with the word
resurrection and what meaning did he see in this event?
Throughout his letters there is only to be found the terse
formulation of the bare fact: 'He rose from the dead'. What
does that mean?

First of all it must be stressed: Paul regarded the resurrection
of Jesus as a *mighty deed of God*. Paul can more or less define God
as the one who can call the dead to life just as in the beginning
he created all from nothing by his mighty summons (Rom.
4:17). That coincides exactly with Judaism's belief about
God—

'Praised art Thou, Jehovah . . . who quickenest the dead . . .'
(Eighteen Benedictions, Second Benediction:

Shemone Esre).

Old Testament belief is aware of this immediate omnipotence of God as the basis of all existing reality. The entirety of the universe would fall apart into nothingness if God were to withdraw his creative power (cf. Ps. 33:4, 6, 8f). It is through God's continuing goodness that men live, birds find their food, flowers bloom (Matt. 6:25ff). None of all that can be taken as a matter of course. Old Testament piety knows no 'Nature' existing *per se*, knows no eternal indestructible universe, knows no eternal return of everything that happens in accord with some inviolably functioning laws of nature. The 'reality' of the world in which people live is established by the mighty will of God, and God's will constantly is at work, governing freely and immediately, a will with which one cannot reckon, but a will on which one must put one's trust.

Therefore, fundamentally, trust or faith is the sensible attitude most attuned to reality. The world is deeply wonderful, not only at its periphery but above all at its daily centre. For man owes himself and his world to the constancy and loyalty of God, to the unchanging continual steadfastness of God's creative goodness, which grants us life and existence. Resurrection of the dead is therefore for Judaism not at all something so absolutely unheard of, nor something so completely suspect as being unreal, as many of us nowadays feel or think. Admittedly, resurrection of the dead for the Jews too falls into the category of something not to be experienced every day; it belongs to the area of things hoped for from God. But such extraordinary hope is only a consequence arising out of ordinary everyday hope. A person who in everyday life has trust, a belief independent of reality, will have trust in his faith also above and beyond all the frontiers of everything he has hitherto met in his experience. It is against this background of Judaism's beliefs about God that the discussion in primitive

Christianity about the resurrection of Jesus by the mighty act
of God is to be understood.

We will have to consider this context more fully later and
here we only establish briefly that Paul understood the
resurrection of Jesus as God with his creative power calling
the dead Jesus out of his grave to life. Throughout, the
resurrection of Jesus is spoken of as the *raising* of Jesus from
the dead *by God* (cf. Rom. 6:4; 8:11–34; 10:9; 1 Cor. 6:14;
Eph. 1:20; 2 Tim. 2:8; Acts 2:24; 3:15; 4:10; 5:30; 10:40;
13:30–37).

Correspondingly, faith is directed towards *God* and not
towards the risen Christ as such (cf. Rom. 4:24; 2 Cor. 1:9;
4:14; Gal. 1:1; 1 Thess. 1:10; 4:14; 1 Peter 1:21). The
Jewish belief in God who can raise the dead and who will do
so, in Christianity has undergone a final concentration; it has
become belief in God, who *has* raised *Jesus* from the dead. The
raising of Jesus from the dead is God's unique demonstration of
his power.

So the theme of the resurrection of Jesus in the mission
preaching of the apostle is in the framework of a call to
conversion, a call to turn to God. Admittedly in general we do
not learn much from Paul's letters about what he himself was
accustomed to preach in the mission situation. But in one
passage in his earliest letter to the community in Thessalonica,
at least the central themes with which the first mission work
was concerned are mentioned briefly. In a passage where he is
looking back at the foundation of the community which has
taken place just previously, Paul resumes them thus: 'You
turned to God by turning from idols and turning to the living
only true God', and you 'wait expectantly for the appearance
from heaven of his Son Jesus, whom he raised from the dead,
Jesus our deliverer from the terrors of judgment to come'
(1 Thess. 1:9f, NEB). This God, whom Paul proclaimed to the
non-Jews, is the God of the Jews. What Paul says of God in this
passage is nothing different from what the Jewish creed says,
which every Jew in those days prayed every day: 'Hear, O

Israel, the Lord is our God, one Lord, and you must love the Lord your God with all your heart and soul and strength' (Deut. 6:4f, NEB).

If a non-Jew was won for the Jewish synagogue as an interested enquirer, the first and basic requirement was that he adhere to this creed and thus renounce all worship of idols, for the first Commandment reads: 'I am the Lord thy God, which brought thee out of the land of Egypt, from the house of bondage.' 'Thou shalt have none other gods before me.' (Deut. 5:6, AV). As with the call to conversion, so too everything else preached by Paul to the heathens in Thessalonica is in agreement with the Jewish beliefs about God. As for the person who trusts and obeys the one God of Israel, he is assured God will look after his good and his salvation: damnation threatens all others. And the Jew trusts that his God will keep faith with the faithful, but will likewise afflict the disloyal person in his disloyalty. Therefore he expected a great Day of Judgment by God in the future, when God finally will consign all his foes, and those who have not been loyal, to eternal destruction; and on the other hand will fulfil his promise of salvation to all who have remained loyal to him. Thus the call to turn to the One God is linked with the warning of the imminent *terrors of the judgment to come,* the judgment through which alone that person will freely pass who turns to God now.

The Jewish mission preachers of the time did not proclaim this any differently from Paul. Compared with the Jewish synagogue, only one thing is new: the proclamation and preaching of the resurrection of Jesus through God's mighty act. In Chapter 2 it will have to be shown more fully that in Judaism the expectation was that, when God's great Day of Judgment fell upon the world, to summon to judgment *all* people without exception, then too not a single one of the dead would escape it either. God would raise the dead from their graves, in order to scrutinize them, and, as with the living, to separate the faithful from those who were disloyal, and consign the unfaithful to eternal destruction, and destine the others for eternal salvation. When now the Christians preached that God *had* raised Jesus from the dead, this meant that God in the case of this One unique person had already accomplished the resurrection process expected at the end of time. For Jewish thinking, the belief in the resurrection of Jesus having taken place implies that God, in advance of his verdict at the day of judgment, already declared that this unique person belongs to him, and therefore has transported him to that eternal life *of full salvation* to that life which he has intended all his people to have.

The function of the risen Lord is that he stands in Heaven ready to save those who believe from the terrors of judgment to come (1 Thess. 1:10, NEB). Therefore, those who have turned to God in obedience ought to profess their allegiance to this Jesus. At the baptism of the Christians newly won over by mission they profess their allegiance: (1) to God, as being He who raised Jesus from the dead, and accordingly, (2) to Jesus, as the 'Lord' whom God appointed through the resurrection:

> 'If on your lips is the confession, "Jesus is Lord" and in your heart the faith that God raised him from the dead then you will find salvation.' (Rom. 10:9, NEB).

The resurrection of Jesus was not preached as an event which only affected Jesus himself, but as an event concerning also the relationship between God and men at the end of time, concerning man's eternal salvation or damnation. Through his resurrection Jesus was appointed to an official position, to that of Saviour of those who belong to God. Since the resurrection, God has transferred to the risen Jesus the operation of his redeeming act at the Day of Salvation, as he has promised those who are faithful to him: and Jesus, since the resurrection, is for God's faithful what God himself is to his people, namely 'The Lord'.

The Christian confession of faith in, and of allegiance to,

Jesus, the Lord (Rom. 10:9), corresponds word for word with Israel's profession of faith in God 'the Lord' (Deut. 6:4, as above). The risen Lord is, so to speak, the mandatory ruler, the authorized agent and representative of God. He is thus celebrated in a hymn which probably originates from the baptismal liturgy of the Pauline Christian communities:

> 'Therefore God raised him to the heights and bestowed on him the name above all names, that at the name of Jesus every knee should bow—in heaven, on earth, and in the depths—and every tongue confess, "Jesus Christ is Lord", to the glory of God the Father.' (Phil. 2:9–11, NEB).

In this hymn a picture is revealed which is tremendous and impressive: a scene in Heaven, high above, in the realm of the throne of God, the ruler over all other powers. All these powers have assembled and are standing before him, ranged according to celestial, earthly or underworld sphere of influence. In this the primitive Christian hymn corresponds to the world picture of the Ancient Orient, according to which the earth is a disc, above which exist the celestial spheres of influence of the divine stellar and planetary powers, who from above exert their power on earth through the means of the earthly rulers and their armies; at the same time, in the water under the disc of the earth the primitive powers exist, against whose resistance earth was once founded, and who therefore from time immemorial are scheming earth's downfall. Superior to all of them in power, God sits on his throne in sublime elevation. The spatial elevation is in keeping with the superiority of his power over all other rulers. And now God enters, leading by the hand Jesus, whom he has raised from death on earth to his side, and God confers on Jesus in the presence of the assembly of all powers of the universe a 'name'. In this connection it must be remembered that in antiquity the name of a person, particularly the name of a ruler, was regarded as a *power-containing medium*. In the name which a person bears there is present the power at his disposal.

He can make this power effective in every word he speaks, in
every command he gives. Accordingly, in the name which God
has conferred on the risen Lord, God has transferred to him his
power. 'The name which is above all other names' is the name
of God, the Lord, alone.

Therefore at this moment of the heavenly investiture of
Christ as Lord with God, all the powers of all the cosmos fall
down before the one so singled out and pay homage to him
with the gesture of subjection, by paying the tribute of
recognizing his name: 'Yes, Jesus Christ is Lord.'

The Letter to the Hebrews depicts the installation of the
risen Lord on the right hand of God in Heaven in a similar way
(Hebr. 1:1ff); God leads him before the choir of angels with
the words of the second Psalm: 'Thou art my Son: today I have
begotten thee' (Hebr. 1:5; cf. 5:5). 'Son' is here used in the
sense of legal status, and this is specifically expressed in the
same Epistle later, where it says that the Son is, alongside the
Father, the Lord over the whole house (Hebr. 3:6). As the son,
Christ inherits God's power over the universe (Hebr. 1:2):
that is to say, what the hymn in the Letter to the Philippians
expressed in one of the names of God, the name 'Lord', is here
described as the legal status of the 'Son', who stands beside the
Father and participates in the power of the Father delegated
to him.

Jesus thus *became* the Son in this sense through his resurrection.
We are here being acquainted with the attitude to Christ which
was the viewpoint held in the earliest period. Christ was spoken
of as the Son of God, not in view of his birth (Luke 1:35) but in
view of his installation as God's mandatory agent at God's
right hand in heaven. That the dignity of the status of being
God's Son was actually meant in this sense, is shown even more
clearly at another passage, where once again Paul is quoting
tradition of the earliest period, namely in Rom. 1:3f. This
passage is a two-part formulation of an article of faith which
contrasts the function of Jesus during his earthly lifetime with
his function in heaven since his resurrection:

(Jesus Christ, our Lord),

I   'born of David's stock according to the flesh,
II   placed in the position of power as the Son of God,
     according to the Holy Spirit, by his resurrection from
     the dead.'

That is to say: as a man on earth Jesus was the Messiah of David's line; through his resurrection Jesus was elevated to the position of power of the Son of God.

Paul himself however blurs the original associations of these statements by placing them both under the heading: The Gospel of his (God's) Son. For, to Paul, Jesus has been from all eternity the Son of God, and as such sent by God down into human existence (cf. Gal. 4:4; Rom. 8:3). In Rom. 1:3f, this view of Jesus's *eternal* Sonship of God is inconsistent with the older view expressed in the formulation taken over by Paul. It is precisely by this discrepancy however that we can recognize the great antiquity of the formulation and its Christology with its view that Jesus was made the Son of God through his resurrection. 'Son of God' was here primarily a designation of his legal status and the corresponding power.

From this we gain a surprising insight into the oldest interpretation of the resurrection of Jesus as such. The resurrection was conceived not as the return of Jesus after his death on the cross to earthly life, but as his elevation into his position of power *in heaven* as the Son of God to whom all powers had been delegated. What we nowadays are accustomed to differentiate, namely, Jesus's resurrection and his ascension, were in the view of the oldest Christology, one and the same thing. For this earliest Christology, the resurrection of Jesus as such was his elevation to heaven to the right hand of God. And the earliest view of the resurrection stresses not so much that he came to life as that God elevated the risen Lord into the heavenly position of power, as the Lord who in the future Last Judgment would pronounce the final verdict on all persons and all powers. The resurrection and the status of son, the name of

Lord and the function as Saviour at the end of time, all belong directly together, for the risen Lord and God belong together. Therefore, belief in God who raised Jesus from the dead is bound up with hope, of the winning, at the end of time, of eternal life and salvation, for those who are the Lord's. For, a person who, in belief in the risen Jesus as the Lord, belongs to him, also trusts Christ, in whom God showed his creative power to awaken the dead, to carry out his promise to bring about the salvation of his own people. The act of entrusting oneself in faith, and the confident hope of salvation, both look in the same direction: they look heavenward, to 'Heaven' where according to the picture in the baptismal hymn, in Phil. 2:9–11, the Risen One has entered on his universal Lordship over all powers. Alone from the domination of this One person depends the salvation at the end of time of those Christians who in baptism have placed themselves under his name.

This is also expressed by another baptismal hymn which is contained in the opening of the First Letter of Peter (1 Peter 1:3–5). The author of the letter continues by speaking of the meaning of this faith for his contemporary situation; namely, even if the Christians are at present experiencing so much hostility from the world around them, to the extent that their faith only earns them suffering and scorn meantime, nevertheless they know that despite this their destiny is secure in the hands of God, and they know in view of the resurrection of Jesus that God's power to salvation is mightier than even death itself. That is why believers can be jubilant in the midst of their suffering (1 Peter 1:6–9). Paul says the same:

'Let us exult in the hope of the divine splendour that is to be ours. More than this: let us even exult in our present sufferings, because we know that suffering trains us to endure, and endurance brings proof that we have stood the test, and this proof is the ground of hope. Such a hope is no mockery, (because God's love has flooded our inmost heart through the Holy Spirit he has given us).' (Rom. 5:2–5, NEB).

'Who will be the accuser of God's chosen ones? It is God who pronounces acquittal; then who can condemn? It is Christ—Christ who died, and, more than that, was raised from the dead—who is at God's right hand, and indeed pleads our cause. Then what can separate us from the love of Christ? Can affliction or hardship? Can persecution, hunger, nakedness, peril, or the sword? . . . For I am convinced that there is nothing in death or life, in the realm of spirits or superhuman powers, in the world as it is or the world as it shall be, in the forces of the universe, in heights or depths—nothing in all creation that can separate us from the love of God in Christ Jesus our Lord'—(that love which has come into effect and is still coming)—(Rom. 8:33–39).

A final confidence capable of supporting burdens of life is here expressed, a confidence which shows endurance in the face of the threatening aspects to be encountered in every earthly existence. This confidence is founded on the clear demonstration of the creative power of God's reliability in the resurrection of Jesus. Just as God overcame the destructive power of death, so too God will accomplish his salvation which he has promised to all his chosen ones despite all the powers of destruction which are at work in the world. In the statements we have quoted hitherto, the death of Jesus appears only as the power of damnation overcome by God (cf. 1 Cor. 15:26). Paul has now tried to bring together in his thinking the statement, in the tradition concerning the Last Supper, which spoke of the power of atonement and reconciliation of the death of Christ (1 Cor. 11:24f; 15:3; see above), and the statement about his resurrection as the demonstration of God's saving power.

Additionally, and in particular, in the Cross of Christ, Paul thus recognizes a demonstration of one aspect of God's *power*: the demonstration of his *love*. By the act of taking upon himself the death which sinners have incurred by their actions (2 Cor. 5:21), Christ, the Just One, has shown his love for them (Gal. 2:20); for 'There is no greater love than this, that a man should lay down his life for his friends.' (John 15:13, NEB).

Love wants to risk involvement for the good of the loved one, even at the cost of its own death. Whereas this seldom occurs among people, and only in exceptional cases (Rom. 5:7f), and people are then only prepared to die for the good they see in their friend; Christ, the Just One, has given his life for the unjust, that is for God's foes.

Paul, in trying to think out the statement of faith handed down by tradition, reasons that God did not abandon Christ, the Just One, that is the one belonging to God, in this situation. Quite on the contrary, God identified himself with Christ: it was God himself who allowed his son to become a man in order to die for the atoning of the sins of men (Rom. 8:3). In Christ's death, therefore, God's love simultaneously came into effect (Rom. 5:8). God's loyalty to those who are loyal to him is extended a stage deeper, and Christ's death shows love to those who are not loyal to him.

God wanted to suspend their wickedness by the only power which can annihilate evil without destroying the people doing the evil, namely, by the power of love (Rom. 12:21). God's love wanted to liberate the evil-doers from the evil to which they had fallen prey by their actions. Thus Paul understood the Cross of Christ as the event in which God showed his *justice and righteousness as love* (Rom. 3:21ff). When Paul speaks of the resurrection of Christ, keeping in mind Christ's death on the cross interpreted in this way, then this implies that Paul understands God's demonstration of *power* in his *act of* resurrection as a demonstration of the *power* of *love*. The creative power of God, which was shown in the abolition of death in the case of Christ, is thus no longer simply to be seen on its own as a pure demonstration of power, but must be seen as love with its redeeming intention. God's omnipotence is thus defined as the power of love.

However, at the same time, the character of the resurrection of Christ as a demonstration of God's power is by no means suspended by the reference to the Cross! Paul does not wish after all to preach only that love sacrifices itself, but that love has the power to carry into effect what love intends to achieve by its sacrifice. Paul's interpretation of the resurrection of Jesus from the meaning of the crucifixion does not imply any resignation; as if coming to nothing were a mark of religious nobility. It is rather the love of the Crucified One which makes the Cross the permanent sign symbolizing all Christianity, including belief in the resurrection. For this very reason, the message of the Cross of Christ belongs together with that of his resurrection, and requires it. For, in the resurrection of Christ the question has been answered as to the *power* of the love of the Crucified One, and its ability to *effectuate* the redeeming intention of that love towards the person loved.

Just as belief in the Resurrected One would be robbed of its decisive criterion if it were not expressly the Crucified One, whose resurrection was being spoken of, so too, conversely, any belief which, together with the message of resurrection, restricted itself to the Cross, would be robbed of its power; for only one who believes in the Resurrected One can see the salvation of the world as founded in Christ's death on the Cross. True salvation in the Christian sense is to be obtained through no other power than the power of love. But there can only be true salvation since through Jesus's resurrection divine proof has been given that love is all-powerful. Power without love brings destruction; but love without power is ineffectual. The preaching of Christ's death on the Cross and his resurrection is, practically speaking, the preaching of the demonstrable power of the love of God which will not abandon one single person to the destructive power of evil, but will free all people from evil, and redeem them for what is good in a life of salvation.

3. ACCOUNTS OF THE RESURRECTION IN THE GOSPELS
(a) *Mark 16 : 1–8*

At the conclusion of the story of the Passion of Jesus, Mark, the earliest evangelist, narrates that after Jesus died on the Cross (not surrounded by any of the disciples, but only by a

crowd of Galilean women followers) Joseph of Arimathaea, a
member of the High Council, sought audience with Pilate and
asked him to give him the body of Jesus (Mark 15:40f). Pilate
was surprised to hear that Jesus was already dead; so he has the
centurion (15:39) make his report.

Only after the centurion has confirmed the death does the
governor give Joseph leave to take the dead body. Joseph buys
a linen sheet, goes to the place of execution, takes down the
body of Jesus from the beam of the Cross, (wraps him in the
sheet), lays him in a tomb cut out of the rock and rolls a stone
against the entrance (15:42–46). Two of the women previously
mentioned see where he is laid in the tomb (15:47).

Thereafter we read (1) 'When the Sabbath was over, Mary
of Magdala, Mary the mother of James, and Salome bought
aromatic oils intending to go and anoint him. (2) And, very
early (on the first day of the week), on the Sunday morning,
just after sunrise, they came to the tomb (3) and they were
wondering among themselves who would roll away the stone
for them from the entrance to the tomb. (4) (Yet) when they
looked up they saw that the stone, huge as it was, had been
rolled back already. (5) They went into the tomb, where they
saw a youth sitting on the right-hand side, wearing a white
robe; and they were dumbfounded. (6) But he said to them,
"Fear nothing; you are looking for Jesus of Nazareth, who was
crucified. He has been raised again; he is not here. Look, here
is the place where they laid him! (7) But go and give this
message to his disciples and Peter: He is going on before you
into Galilee; there you will see him, as he told you!" (8) Then
they dashed out and ran away from the tomb, beside themselves
with terror. They said nothing to anybody, for they were
afraid.' (Mark 16:1–8, NEB).

We must not make the mistake of immediately seeing this
narrative from our point of view, as if we were considering a
present-day report. We must rather, first of all, attempt to
adopt the narrator's viewpoint in order to perceive what it was
his intention to stress. Seen in this light, one thing is immediately

clear: the objective of the whole narrative complex is to stress the message of the angel proclaiming the raising from the dead of the Crucified One. The narrative's structure curving upwards to this objective incorporates the account of the burial of Jesus at the centre of which is the short description of his being laid in the tomb (15:46). The previously related episode with Pilate (15:44ff) was missing in the original version; Matthew and Luke evidently did not find it in their copy of the Gospel according to St Mark (cf. Matt. 27:58f; Luke 23:52f). Originally the beginning only mentioned briefly that Joseph requested Pilate for the body of Jesus for burial. All the stress is laid on the carrying out of the burial. However, in the description (15:46), it strikes the reader that the narrator would like to direct attention to the tomb in the rock with the stone sealing the entrance.

Admittedly, mention of the grave linen shows that we are thinking of a proper burial; there is no question of a hasty makeshift arrangement. But it is not the burial as such which the narrator wishes to emphasize, but only the fact that the tomb was firmly sealed. From this it can be recognized that already the following story of the angel's message in the opened tomb is the centre of interest. The whole account of the burial of Jesus leads on to the episode, and is leading up to it as its ultimate climax. This objective is served by the added remark about the women (15:47): they are witnesses not of the burial proceedings but of the location of the tomb. So, one can say that the story of the burial of Jesus has as its intention to describe the setting of the Easter story narrated next. This, in its turn, marks the event of the raising from the dead which the angel proclaims, by directing attention to the alteration that has occurred at the tomb: the stone has been rolled away from the entrance (16:4), the body of Jesus is 'not there' (16:6).

One may ask oneself whether the anxious worry of the women on their way to the tomb, wondering who would roll away the stone for them from the entrance to the tomb (16:3f),

is not a later accretion, for in Matthew and Luke this feature is
missing. A later writer may have inserted it in order to
underline the contrast between the closing of the tomb by
human hand and its miraculous opening by God's act of
resurrection. Also the detail, that the women went to the tomb
with the intention, after all, of anointing the body of Jesus
(16:1), could have been added subsequently to the account in
order to give concrete motivation to the women's movements.
That the omission, in the account of the burial, of mention of
anointing of the dead was noticed, is shown by another story
which depicts how before the beginning of his sufferings Jesus
had a large quantity of anointing oil poured over him by a
woman, and how Jesus interpreted this as an anticipation of
the anointing of his body in death for burial (Mark 14:3–8).
So too the intention of the women at the beginning of the
Easter story at Mark 16:1 to anoint the body of Jesus, may be
a later addition. Matthew and Luke evidently felt the uneven
flow in the account of the burial.

The former, therefore, only speaks of the desire of the women
to 'see' Jesus once again (Matt. 28:1). Luke, on the other hand,
has the women buy anointing oils already on the evening of the
burial, and stresses that because of onset of the Sabbath they
were not able to go to the tomb till the morning of the first day
of the week (Luke 23:54–24:1). In this way he allows the
impression to arise that the anointing by the women should
belong to the burial itself, and had only to be delayed for a day
in order to keep the legal observance of the Sabbath. It is also
to be supposed that the Easter story in Mark was considerably
shorter at the beginning in its original version. But also in its
present filled-out form it clearly concentrates on the scene in
the tomb. What the women want, and why they are worried, is
unimportant, after all, the moment they are confronted by the
angel's proclamation announcing the extraordinary miracle
that has taken place. This proclamation is the real nucleus of
the story. Now, in the angel's message alongside the proclamation of the resurrection of Christ (16:6) there is the instruction

to the women to command the disciples to go to encounter him in Galilee (16:7). The angel bases his command expressly on the previous word of Jesus (14:28): 'After I am raised again I will go on before you into Galilee' (Mark 14:28, NEB). It is very surprising that, after such an announcement beforehand and the express command of the angel, there is no account of this appearance to the disciples in Galilee! Mark's account breaks off with the sentence about the women's terrified flight from the tomb, and that is the end of St Mark's Gospel as a whole. Did the original version relate the scene in Galilee, and was that the original ending of the book which is not preserved in our present text? This conjecture has often been made, on the basis of 14:28 and 16:7. But then one would have to explain why this ending was subsequently broken off. Some commentators are of the opinion that the final piece of the book roll or the last leaf of the original copy could have been lost by external damage. But that is pure speculation unsubstantiated by any observation; furthermore, it is unlikely, since one can hardly assume that this misfortune would happen neatly exactly after the end of the last complete sentence (Mark 16:8), and before the beginning of the first sentence on the next scene. If a page is torn off, the tear is generally through the middle of a sentence, indeed through the middle of a word. Therefore other commentators suppose that the final scene in Galilee was deliberately removed. However, the reasons suggested for this are not very convincing. For example, one suggestion is that it was wished to avoid the doubling of the places, Jerusalem and Galilee, and to concentrate all the Easter events uniformly in Jerusalem.

Indeed, the later tradition in Luke and John, shows that the appearances of the Risen One had been transferred to Jerusalem. But why should Mark or his later editor not already have done likewise instead of just scoring out the whole story because of the geographical reference—a story furthermore which deals with the disciples, who are annoyingly absent in the scene at the tomb! For such an incisive drastic operation there must have been, quite definitely, more important, more compelling grounds!

Therefore other commentators, in their turn, suspect that the story of the appearance in Galilee was deleted in order to conceal the shameful flight of the disciples. But this intention also could have been carried out much more convincingly by Mark, in the way Luke and John have done: they relate, namely, that the women immediately reported their experience at the tomb to the disciples and that the Risen One then appeared to them as the first witnesses. Furthermore it can be objected that anyone only wanting to retouch the shameful flight of the disciples would have achieved his purpose better in any other way than by deleting the very story dealing with the disciples; for such a deletion would surely have directly provoked the question as to the whereabouts of the disciples in connection with the Easter events. Both express references to the meeting of the disciples with Jesus in Galilee (14:28 and 16:7) fulfil the very purpose of *pointing to* the disciples. Anyone wanting to retouch the account of Jesus's appearance in the disciples' presence, would not have let these references stand, far less have added another of his own. In addition, he could have achieved his purpose much more simply and effectively than by carrying out all such operations on the Easter story, if he had just deleted the one offending sentence about the flight of the disciples (Mark 14:50)—as Luke had done (Luke 23:53–54).

So there remains only one last argument usually brought forward to account for the replacement of an original story of an appearance of the risen Lord by the substitution of the story of the empty tomb: in order to remove any doubt about the reality of the resurrection of Jesus, more dramatic presentation was required at the end of the Passion story than the story telling only of one appearance of Jesus, but not telling of his resurrection itself. The emphatic stress on the empty tomb would have fulfilled this purpose better in every respect. For, by this reference it was intended that it should be shown that

Jesus who had left his tomb had really risen bodily from the dead. But there is no indication in the wording of the story in Mark 16 that it does in fact follow the tendency of this line of argument. Surely the angel pointing to the empty tomb, in verse 6, is giving support to the proclamation of the resurrection.

But the accentuation lies on the fact that the One crucified by *men* has been raised from the dead by *God* (cf. 9:31) and so the place where they (!) laid him is now empty. The empty tomb is thus a kind of trophy of God's, symbolizing his victory over the foes of Jesus, who up to his death effectively exerted their power against him, but who with his death have now come to the limit of their power. It is, on the other hand, silent about the *bodily* reality of the resurrection of Jesus. Thus, there is every indication that Mark's Gospel originally contained no final scene in Galilee, either following upon the story of the tomb or in its place. How then is it to be explained why Mark expressly refers to the appearance in Galilee but does not go on to give an account of it? Well, there is a very simple explanation: namely, that Mark did not yet know any detailed *account* of this appearance. He did not know any more about it than Paul at 1 Cor. 15:5, namely, only the fact of the appearance. It has been shown above, that, in the earliest period, the appearances of the Risen One were regarded as evidence of certain persons having received special authority and commission from Jesus himself. Therefore, only the fact of the appearance was handed down in a short sentence in the tradition, because in this context it was only the fact alone which was of interest. The appearances of the Risen One were considered as instances of vocation. Mark knew of the appearance in the presence of the 'disciples and Peter' through the same traditional item of information quoted by Paul at 1 Cor. 15:5. In the story of the tomb as it was handed down to him Mark found no reference as yet to the disciples. However, he did not want the important tidings of the appearance of the Risen One to be missing in the narrative context of the Easter story. So he let Jesus already himself (14:28) point forward to it, and, correspondingly, Mark added to the proclamation of the resurrection by the angel (16:6), the command to the disciples (16:7). His readers could understand both of the references, because, after all, the *fact* of the appearance was known to them as it was to Mark. It was only in the case of Mark's successors that the need arose to amplify the mere reference and expand it into an explanatory account. Matthew did this with consistent thoroughness in that he relates that the women were not silent about what had befallen them, but had recounted it to the disciples (Matt. 28:8). On their way to the disciples the Risen One himself had appeared to them and confirmed his directions to them (Matt. 28:9f): and in the final scene in Matthew's Gospel what was announced is fulfilled. Jesus appears to his eleven disciples on the mountain in Galilee and they 'see' him (28:16–20).

It was thus probably first of all Mark who added the reference to the appearance of the Risen One to his disciples in Galilee at Mark 16:7. Then the conclusion of his account (16:8) becomes a problem; namely, why do the women not obey the command of the angel, but obstinately keep silent about their experience at the tomb? All the later evangelists have reversed this remark, and all recount on the contrary that the women hastened to the disciples, and told them what had happened. Mark only refers to the fear of the women, but Matthew adds mention of their 'great joy' (Matt. 28:8)!

However, the contradiction between the command of the angel in Mark 16:7, and its not being carried out in Mark 16:8, is so clearly and forcibly emphasized that it must be deliberate intention on the part of Mark. It is recognizable what that intention is when one knows the whole of Mark. It is, namely, striking how Mark on several occasions recounts that, after performing miracles, Jesus forbade people to talk about the great miraculous deeds in which he effectively channelled God's power of salvation. He gives a stern warning to the leper who has been healed: 'Be sure you say nothing to anybody' (Mark 1:44; cf. also 7:36). Above all, however, he insists that

Peter's insight, his recognition that he is the Messiah, must not be spread any further (Mark 8:30); only when he had risen from the dead were his disciples permitted to proclaim who Jesus in reality truly is (9:9). The last passage shows that there exists a connection between the remark about the women's silence at Mark 16:8 and the commands of Jesus to be silent.

By rights this was the moment now, after the angel's proclamation of the resurrection at Mark 16:6, when, according to Mark 9:9, it could be openly proclaimed that Jesus the Messiah is the Son of God. Why, therefore, do the women not immediately pass on the angel's message? Now, the reason would seem to be that Mark would like to give prominence to the disciples, and not the women, as the first witnesses to the resurrection. This, in its turn, as we have already seen, is very closely linked with the tradition about the appearance of the Risen One in the presence of his disciples, introduced by Mark (16:7) in the narrative context of the story of the tomb. It is only at his appearance to them that the Risen One authorizes and empowers them to preach the gospel. So Mark at the end of his book indicates where the realization who Jesus really is had its legitimate origin; not in the mouths of the women, but from the lips of the disciples. The women in their fear did not understand the angel's message: so the great tidings still remained hidden. It was only through the appearance of the Risen One himself that these tidings were revealed; and his disciples, with Peter at their head, were those who first proclaimed the tidings!

Here too Matthew expanded what Mark first outlined. Jesus's appearance to the eleven disciples, which Matthew reports at the end of his book (Matt. 28:16–20), is nothing other than their being called to mission to the nations. This conception agrees fully with what we recognized, above, to be the earliest view of the resurrection of Jesus; namely, through his resurrection Jesus had had transferred to him God's divine power: the Risen One is God's representative to the end of

time (Matt. 28:18). In this capacity, Jesus, in appearing to his
disciples, is commissioning them as his authorized emissaries on
earth. If before Easter the disciples had only had Jesus's
message about the Kingdom of God being at hand, and his
demands on his disciples, as topics to proclaim in the villages
and cities of Israel (as Matt. 10:5ff), now the radius of the
mission has expanded worldwide: all nations are to be won as
his disciples and taught to live in accordance with his teaching
(Matt. 28:19).

So, it is possible to trace how the tradition, begun by Mark
and expanded by Matthew, of the appearance of the Risen
One, appearing to authorize and commission his disciples, has
been later linked with the story of the angel's proclamation at
Jesus's tomb of the resurrection. Before Mark the two traditions
were separate and independent of one another: on the one
hand there was the story of the tomb as the Easter conclusion of
the Passion story; on the other hand there was the news of the
appearances of the Risen One, through which specific men
were called to be leaders in the community of disciples of Jesus
and to be missionaries in his name. Mark was first to combine
both different Easter traditions by having the angel proclaim
the fact of the resurrection of Jesus (Mark 16:6) but also
announce the first appearance of the Risen One to his disciples
(16:7). At the end too, he indicated that it was not the women,
but first of all the disciples who broke the silence about the true
nature of Jesus and proclaimed his resurrection. From fear the
women had kept silent about their experience at the tomb
(16:8b). The story before Mark, on the other hand, was not
interested in the Easter *Sermon*: interest was concentrated
wholly on the news of the resurrection as such (16:6).
Accordingly it concluded as Old Testament reports often end
when reporting encounters with God or his angel. The direct
encounter with the Holy One is terrible. Trembling and terror
seize the women, therefore, and they flee from the place where
they have confronted the angel of God (16:8a). There now
follows from this a conclusion which is of great significance for

our entire verdict about the Easter testimony: namely, the story of the empty tomb already belonged to the Easter Conclusion of the account of the Passion in the tradition before Mark. It is necessary here to inform the reader that this verdict about the story of the tomb is by no means unanimously held; and is in fact rather disputed in present-day research. There are many Biblical exegetes who judge it to be of relatively late origin and an apologetic legend which is intended to underline the bodily reality of the resurrection of Jesus by pointing to the empty tomb. Some of the reasons given for this view have already been rejected above as unlikely and therefore untenable.

The suggestion, that the story of the tomb was only subsequently inserted where it now is in Mark's text, has been supported by other arguments which now remain to be examined. These suggested reasons have to do with the linking of the story of the tomb with the narrative context preceding it. Here a number of points can be observed in the texts which would seem to show that the linking is by no means organic and smooth, but rather subsequent patching-together.

First of all: the names of the women, as given in three places, do not coincide (15:40, 47; 16:1), and above all: the sentence 15:47 clashes with the immediately following sentence introducing the story of the tomb 16:1: 'And Mary of Magdala and Mary the mother of Joseph were watching and saw where he was laid. When the Sabbath was over, Mary of Magdala, Mary the mother of James, and Salome bought aromatic oils . . .' Here Matthew removes the discrepancy by merely speaking of two women and naming the second one 'the other Mary' (Matt. 27:61; 28:1).

Many commentators thereupon express the verdict thus: 15:47 is the conclusion of the story of the burial with which originally the story of the Passion of Jesus closed. The story of the empty tomb was originally an independent individual legend. It was only its later addition to the story of the burial which led to the two sentences about the women standing in

such immediate juxtaposition. From this it could be seen that
16:1ff was not originally in the narrative context of the story of
the Passion. Indeed, it is hard to explain, if the narrative
context arose organically, how these two sentences came
together in such a clumsy laborious style. The discrepancy
evidently points, as in many other similar passages in the New
Testament, to the fact that something was subsequently
appended or inserted. However, the explanation just given is
not the only possible one. One can also consider whether,
instead of the whole story of the empty tomb, it was not only
mention of the women, at 16:1, which was later inserted. This
is suggested by the following observation: at the beginning of
the story of the burial (15:42) the detailed time-specification
stands out conspicuously from the narrative context: 'By this
time evening had come; and as it was Preparation Day (that is,
the day before the Sabbath). . . .' By specifying the time, not
only is the death of Jesus fixed on the Friday, but the burial of
Jesus is placed under the urgent pressure of time, because of the
imminent beginning of the Sabbath, on which no pious Jew
may work.

In the account itself then, we must admit, there is no trace
at all of any haste; the fixing of the time on the evening before
the beginning of the Sabbath, in verse 42, is thus probably a
later insertion. Similarly, observance of the rule against work
on the Sabbath is expressed in the emphatic remark in 16:1:
'When the Sabbath is over', that is, by Jewish reckoning, on
the evening after the sun had gone down, the women had
purchased anointing oils. This sounds as if the women are
being protected against the suspicion of having broken the
Sabbath rest by buying the anointing oils. This too could have
been the intention of the subsequent insertion of 16:1. If, for
the sake of experiment, one were to leave it out, the report
would read as follows: The women saw where Jesus had been
laid to rest (15:47), they bought anointing oils in order to
anoint him (16:1b) and they then came early on the morning
of the first day of the week to the tomb (16:2). If the original

narrative context only included this single reference to the day after the Sabbath, it could indeed give the unfortunate impression that the preceding action had broken the Sabbath rest.

Accordingly, in an introduction with new emphasis, express assurance was added that such violation of the Sabbath was excluded, and a second list of names of three women was used (16:1a). Thus, what happened after the end of the Sabbath is clearly separated from what went before. For the same reason, the details specifying the time, at 15:42b, are inserted, in order to stress that the burial took place not on the Sabbath (as one might otherwise wrongly conclude) but on the day before— even if this is not very easy to believe if one begins to work out for oneself how much time must have elapsed from the audience with Pilate in the evening (15:42a), and the buying of the linen for the burial, to the completion of the burial itself (15:46); far too long a period for the burial to have been completed before the beginning of the Sabbath at 6 p.m.

Concentration on the primary concern lest the Sabbath should have been broken, led to the oversight that the additions, as is so often the case with such subsequent inter- polations, did not fit into the narrative context. Incidentally, the introduction of different women's names at 16:1 from the names at 15:47 led to a little retouching at the first mention of the women (15:40f): the second woman is elaborately named as Mary 'mother of James the younger and of Joseph' (NEB);* and the Mary at 15:47 and the Mary at 16:1 are balanced out. Our conclusion is: the two competing groups of names at 15:47 and 16:1 do not force us at all to assume that the story at 16:1–8 was only a later insertion in the narrative context of the Passion story. This allows us to be all the more confident of the conclusion we worked out earlier that what we have is the core of the original Easter ending of the Passion story of Jesus.

* *Translator's note:* Wilckens's original reads, 15:40f 'Mary *wife* of James and *mother* of Joseph'.

(b) *The Account of the Resurrection in the Context of the
    Story of the Passion*

Further confirmation of our judgment is provided, finally,
by the character and the curve of action of the Passion account
preceding it. The story depicts in impressively sober stark
language, how Jesus, arrested at the instigation of the Jewish
leaders, accused on the basis of false testimonies and condemned
to death for his confession to being the Messiah, handed over to
the Roman governor for sentence charged with stirring up
messianic rebellion, condemned by the Roman governor to
death on the Cross, tormented and derided by the soldiery,
nailed to the Cross, and mocked and despised by all the
bystanders, died. Jesus himself from beginning to end is
completely passive, intentionally. Throughout it is the Jewish
leaders who are carrying out the actions. His disciples fail him:
one betrayed him, one denies him and curses him, all of them
take to flight as soon as he has hardly been arrested.

The narrative leaves absolutely not the slightest doubt that
terrible injustice is being perpetrated. Jesus is not only
innocent, a victim sacrificed to the angry hatred of the masses:
but above all, it is the Messiah, God's Son, on whom this
injustice is being inflicted. Jesus himself confesses who he is,
unambiguously and publicly, both before the highest court of
the Jews (Mark 14:61f) and before the Roman governor
(Mark 15:2). So it is the representative of God among men,
who is at the mercy of their injustice (cf. 9:31). In complete
isolation he stands up for God's cause. And his intentional
stance of passivity provokes the reader to ask where God was in
all this increasing injustice? 'My God, my God, why hast thou
forsaken me?'—these are the last words of the Crucified One
(15:34f).

The Passion story thus contains enormous tension—*God's*
representative in the hands of *men* (14:41)! This tension is
intentional; in fact the account is so structured that the tension
rises step by step. Closer observation shows that the entire
happening of the Passion corresponds to the Old Testament

picture of the suffering Just One, who appears in a group of Psalms, crying for justice and help. This correspondence is revealed down to the individual stations. The last cry of Jesus is the beginning of Psalm 22, from which also other individual features of the Passion narrative are taken (cf. Mark 15:24 with Ps. 22:18; Mark 15:29 with Ps. 22:8f). It would go beyond the limits of this study to quote all such parallels. The reader may care to compare:

Mark 14:1 with Ps. 37:32; 54:3 and 86:14;
Mark 14:18 with Ps. 41:9 (cf. John 13:18);
Mark 14:66ff with Ps. 55:12–15;
Mark 14:50 with Ps. 38:11;
Mark 14:56 with Ps. 27:12; 35:11; 109:1–5;
Mark 14:60f with Ps. 38:12–14; 39:9; Is. 53:7–12 (cf. Luke 23:24);
Mark 15:36 with Ps. 69:21.

The great number of such allusions, to the Old Testament Psalms on suffering, clearly shows that the Passion story of Jesus, for certain stretches, is completely taken from the Old Testament. The Christians, who structured this report, evidently recognized in the path of suffering of their Lord the paradigm of the Just One in the Psalms. Only thus were they able to understand what atrocity has been perpetrated on Jesus. In this understanding there is also contained a verdict reached about Jesus himself: Jesus is the Just One of God; precisely in his suffering he belonged to God, and therefore he completely left it to God what would become of himself.

The challenge, which, according to Psalm 22:8, his foes call out triumphantly: 'He threw himself on the Lord for rescue; let the Lord deliver him, for he holds him dear!' (Ps. 22:8) is—only turned into the positive—the assumption underlying the account by the early Christians of the suffering of Jesus: what Christ's opponents did to him, they did to God. This results in the enormous tension which runs throughout the Passion story increasing from station to station till it reaches its climax in the

last cry of Jesus with the words of the Psalm. Has God
abandoned his Just One? Is that the point of the old account of
the Passion? Or is it at least the question which is so solidly and
brutally worked out in it, in order that it should remain a
burning question for Christians of all centuries?

It is impossible to be a disciple of Christ, as understood by
those Christians of the earliest period, unless one sees in him
the representative of the God of Israel, and unless one therefore
also sees the story of his Passion as a story of enormous
blasphemy. Flagrant injustice is perpetrated against this man—
where is God? It is part of the character of those Old Testament
Psalms of suffering that the hopeless distress of the complaint of
the Just One is followed by the hymn of praise of the Saved
One (cf. e.g. Ps. 22:22ff; 69:30ff).

That God himself is 'Just' and helps his Just Ones, rescues
them out of the hands of their foes and does not let them be
mocked, is a basic motif of Israelite faith; and, as such, the
assumption underlying all prayers of lamentation handed down
in tradition. However, if one seeks in the Passion story these
statements about salvation found in the Psalms, or at least if
one is looking for motifs indicating confidence in salvation, the
search is in vain. The events roll on without any sign of divine
intervention.

The representative of God is entirely at the mercy of the
arbitrary behaviour of his foes. He is abandoned by all, totally
alone. The harshness of the account is quite unmitigated. Yet
nowhere is there a tone of resignation or bitterness. Throughout,
the report is guided by the clear simple conviction that Jesus
belongs to God, that it is as God's representative that he is
enduring all suffering, indeed that the suffering is happening to
him in accordance with God's will.

The account of Jesus's prayer in the garden of Gethsemane
(Mark 14:32ff) emphasizes exactly this: 'Yet not what I will,
but what thou wilt' (Mark 14:36, NEB). In his suffering there is
fulfilled what is said in the Old Testament about his destiny
(Mark 14:49): he 'had to undergo great sufferings' (Mark

8:31). How can this inner tension, between the unrestrained harshness of the suffering reported and this certain clear conviction of the divine right of Jesus, be explained? The answer can only be that the Christians, who reported the path of suffering of their Lord, knew of his resurrection. For this very reason, all the salvation motifs found in the Psalms about suffering are missing in the account of Jesus's Passion, because the community, in which and for which the account was narrated, saw in the resurrection of Jesus the decisive concentrated response of God to the injustice committed against his representative. In raising Jesus from the dead, from the death which his foes had brought upon him, God had cancelled out their unjust deed. Death is the limit of their power over him. They were able to kill him—but they could not destroy him! For God's power had revealed itself beyond this limit, demonstrated on the one they had killed. His tomb is the authentication of his triumph over his foes: 'the place where they laid him' (Mark 16:6) is empty. This also is to say that the Easter story, at Mark 16:1–8, in the narrative context of the Passion story, has this very function: it marks God's response to the blasphemous actions of men against his representative, and it is simultaneously an answer to the question about God's whereabouts in view of his suffering. Where the Psalms about suffering speak of the final saving of the suffering Just One by God's help, at the end of the story of the Passion of Jesus, the Just One, the divine messenger of God proclaims Christ's resurrection as his saving through God's mighty act. Now it is proven that Jesus's confession before the High Council (Mark 14:62) is not blasphemy but is the truth: Jesus is the Messiah, the Son of the Living God; his foes will not see him again until he appears at the Last Judgment (cf. Mark 13:26ff; Matt. 23:39). That is evidently the concept which is linked in the angel's proclamation of the earliest Easter story (Mark 16:6) with his rising from the dead. It is vain to look for 'Jesus of Nazareth, who was crucified' in the tomb. 'He has been raised again; he is not here'; he is not at 'the place where they laid him', but on the contrary he is with God.

In this sense the story in Mark 16:1–8, in its original form
(vv. 2–6, 8a) constitutes the conclusion of the ancient account
of the Passion. Such a conclusion is required by the inner
structure and 'profile' of the narrative. It is required for two
further reasons. It is necessary because it is impossible to
envisage what function a straightforward account of the
Passion could be intended to fulfil in the religious life of
the community handing on such a tradition, if it did not
conclude with a mention of the resurrection of Jesus at his
death. Such a conclusion is required, too, for the more
important reason that the picture of the Suffering Jesus
corresponds to the picture of the Suffering Jewish One, and
one important detail of this picture is that God saves the Man
of Sorrows from all his suffering.

But if one has to postulate such an Easter conclusion to the
Passion story, then no other conclusion can be substituted for
the story of the tomb, and analysis of the story has after all
shown that it forms the earliest obtainable Easter conclusion of
the Passion account.

Finally it must be stressed: however much the resurrection
occurrence is central to the story, nevertheless it is not depicted.
Its occurrence is taken for granted. However much the
resurrection message of the angel stresses the occurrence of
the resurrection as God's deed through which the effect of men's
blasphemous deed is cancelled, it is far from being concerned
with proving the resurrection as a 'fact'. The empty tomb is not
intended as a proof of the resurrection, and certainly not as
evidence of the physical bodily reality of the resurrection of
Jesus. The empty tomb is for the narrator completely un-
disputed, and it serves him as a trophy of the victory over those
who set out to murder Jesus and to destroy him.

(c) *Elaboration in the Gospels after Mark*

Regarding the later expansions of the Easter story after
Mark, above all, three additions must be mentioned briefly.

The *first* comes from Matthew who has woven into Mark's narrative context a parallel self-contained story which he evidently knew from a separate special tradition (Matt. 27:62–66; 28:2–4, 11–15). The story recounts that the Jewish leaders had approached Pilate and had demanded and been given a military guard for the tomb of Jesus, in order to deprive the disciples of any chance of stealing their Master's body and then saying that he had arisen from the dead. Yet these soldiers are cast to the ground by the appearance of the angel on Easter morning so that the angel can, unhindered, roll away the stone from the entrance to the tomb, and seat himself upon it. After everything is over, the soldiers hasten to the Jewish leaders and report the incident and the leaders bribe them to say when questioned that the disciples of Jesus had secretly stolen his body while they had nodded off to sleep. And in this way rumour has survived 'till the present day'. 'This story became widely known, and is current in Jewish circles to this day' (Matt. 28:15). From this last sentence it becomes clear what the objective of this story has been all along (27:63f): it wishes to contradict an evil rumour spread by the Jewish leaders, suggesting that the Christian story of the resurrection was based on a wicked deception by the disciples.

It is easy for us nowadays to see in it the product of naive unsubtle massive polemic, but for the Christians under attack the accusation must have appeared dangerous at the time. So it is to be explained that their retaliation was similar; and in their turn they now attributed to the Jewish leaders evil, cunning, polemics and counter-polemics. In every age there is a habit of escalating the absurdity of the arguments. It is only of interest to us that the Jewish polemics did not argue about the empty tomb as such, but accepted it from Christian tradition as a given fact.

From this it can be inferred that the story of the empty tomb can not have only been known since Mark, but must have already belonged, for a considerable time previously, to the established Christian tradition. If even the slightest trace could

have been found to show that on the Christian side the story
was one which had only just arisen, then it is quite certain that
the Jewish polemics would not have let slip the opportunity to
unhinge a hated belief and discredit the heretics' faith in the
resurrection. The same story incidentally is to be found,
without anti-Jewish apologetics, in the apocryphal mid-second-
century Gospel of Peter. The individual details are there, but
even more unsubtle; a sort of heavenly-earthly drama, told for
the naive astonishment of the Christian rank-and-file, taking
naive pleasure in the shiver of awe at the miraculous.

A *second* expansion of the Easter story is given in the Gospels
according to St Luke and St John. Here it is reported that the
three women had immediately reported their discovery to
the gathered disciples, who had initially dismissed it as women's
confused idle talk (Luke 24:11). For all that, Peter did,
however, run to the tomb, saw only all the grave-clothes lying
there in the opened tomb, and returned full of astonishment
(Luke 24:12–24). ('Peter, however, got up and ran to the
tomb, and, peering in, saw the wrappings and nothing more;
and he went home amazed at what had happened' (Luke
24:11c).)

In St John's Gospel this same story has been expanded later.
There two of the disciples, Peter and the unnamed 'disciple
whom Jesus loved', compete racing to the tomb. The
favourite disciple gets there first, but waits for Peter who is first
to enter the burial chamber and sees lying there the wrappings
and the napkin (which had been over the head). After Peter,
the other disciple went in too, 'and he saw and believed'
(John 20:1–9). Instead of the shocked wonder, as in Luke,
here belief is the reaction to the discovery of the empty tomb,
which does the 'beloved' disciple credit in the presence of
Peter. Probably the evangelist wishes to include him in his
sketch as a perfect disciple, as a representative pre-figuring
later Christian believers.

In the narrative as it reached Luke and John the essential
point is to reinforce the testimony of the women with that of the

disciples (cf. Luke 24:24). But their discovery does not bring about belief: on the contrary the narrative goes so far as to construct a contrast between the objective establishment of the facts, from the reader's aspect, and the sheer incomprehension on the part of the disciples actually involved. Their discovery only has the force of proof for the community of believers, for whom the story is told.

Finally, a *third* amplification of the tomb scene is found in Matthew and John where there is an account of an appearance of Jesus to the women on their way to the disciples. Whereas however in Matthew (28:9f) the risen Christ only appears to confirm personally the angel's directions to the disciples (v. 7); in John's account, the story stresses Mary Magdalena's experience itself. She is standing weeping at the grave since she can only infer from the tomb being empty that the body of Jesus has in the meantime been moved to another resting place (John 20:2). First of all she pours out her grief to two angels she sees sitting in the burial chamber (vv. 11–13) then asks Jesus himself, whom she takes to be the gardener, whither the body has been taken (v. 14f). Then he calls her by her name, and she recognizes him and she wants to fall at his feet (v. 16; cf. Matt. 28:9). Yet he does not allow her to touch him, but charges her to report to the disciples that he is now ascending to his heavenly Father. This much discussed strange remarkable injunction not to touch the risen Christ is probably inserted by the evangelist into the story of the appearance as he found it.

The object of the original story was to tell of their recognition of Jesus and the women's adoring homage. In John's judgment this is not yet due to the risen Christ at this moment. Christ is, namely, on his way to heaven, and it is only as the transfigured Christ, the glorified Lord, that it is seemly for him to receive the adoration and veneration of his 'real worshippers' (cf. 4:23f). It can be clearly recognized that this narrative of Christ's appearance has only been added later to the Easter story of the empty tomb and is only intended to corroborate the angel's proclamation of the resurrection through confirmation by the risen Christ himself. The women are not told to do anything more than to pass on the message to the disciples. They are not given any kind of special revelation. That is only the case in the later gospel writings from gnostic-heretical circles. It is only there that the clearly maintained differentiation in the Biblical tradition between the women and the disciples is first set aside and the women become privileged favoured recipients of heavenly secrets.

### 4. GOSPEL ACCOUNTS OF APPEARANCES OF THE RISEN CHRIST

#### (a) *Christ's Appearances as Call to Vocation (Matt. 28: 16–20)*

Our examination of the Easter story in Mark has shown that before Mark the story had no connection with appearances of the risen Christ. The angel on his own was fully valid authority for the proclamation of what happened at Easter. In telling of the injunction to the disciples (Mark 16:7), it was Mark himself who added the first hint of a continuation of the Easter happening in an appearance of Christ to 'the disciples and Peter', and at the same time too it was Mark who devalued the role of the women as compared to the disciples by his remark (Mark 16:8b) about the silence of the women. In as much as Jesus appeared to the disciples, this established them, and not the women, as the legitimate preachers of the message of the resurrection.

Matthew elaborated this hint. In his version he has the risen Christ, in his appearance to the women, confirm the commission to his disciples; and then Matthew gives an account of this appearance to the disciples in Galilee as the actual real climax of the Easter story (Matt. 28:16ff). The scene has two parts. Firstly there is a short description of the eleven disciples going to Galilee and climbing the mountain to which Jesus ordered them to go. There the disciples see Jesus and fall prostrate before him. Thus what was foretold in 28:7 and 10 is fulfilled. 'Yet some of them doubted' (Matt. 28:17). This refers to their hesitation because of lack of faith (Matt. 14:28–31). That these disciples are of such 'little faith' is not remedied by their seeing Jesus but only by the mission he entrusts to them. So the risen Christ's words to the disciples form the middle part of the scene (Matt. 28:18–20). The first part is merely the introduction to it.

Jesus first of all introduces himself in the position he occupies as the risen Christ: 'Full authority in heaven and on earth has been committed to me' (Matt. 28:18). This is an allusion to the vision of the 'Son of Man' in the Book of Daniel: 'I was still watching in visions of the night and I saw one like a man coming with the clouds of heaven; he approached the Ancient in Years and was presented to him. Sovereignty and glory and kingly power were given to him, so that all people and nations of every language should serve him; his sovereignty was to be an everlasting sovereignty which should not pass away, and his kingly power such as should never be impaired' (Dan. 7:13–14, NEB). This is how Matthew understood Jesus's presentation of himself: as the risen Christ he has been placed by God in the key position of heavenly power. This is the same conception as is also to be found in the pre-Pauline Confession which we commented on above (Rom. 1:4): 'he was declared Son of God by a mighty act in that he rose from the dead' (NEB). So Matthew too interpreted the resurrection of Jesus in the sense of the earliest Christology, namely, as Christ's being carried off into heaven and being installed in an incomparable position of power with God. In all this dignity of his heavenly position of honour he appears to his disciples. But this conception is for its part only the introduction to the task set them in his command: 'Go forth therefore and make all nations my disciples; baptize men everywhere in the name of the Father and the Son and the Holy Spirit, and teach them to observe all that I have commanded you' (Matt. 28:19–20).

The risen Christ is thereby installing his disciples as missionaries, handing over to them the very task of preaching on which he himself had till then been engaged. On the same mountain on which he had proclaimed his teaching (Matt.

5:1ff) he now gives his disciples full authority to preach his teaching among all nations. And as they henceforth are to represent him, he assures them of his continuing presence 'always, to the end of time' (Matt. 28:20). The appearance of Jesus is thus an act of sovereignty at the sending of his disciples on their divine mission. On this point too Matthew agrees with the earliest understanding of the appearance of the risen Christ. Thus Matthew's account belongs to the earlier phase of the history of the traditions concerning the appearance of the risen Christ.

(b)  *His Appearances as Identification of Jesus* (*Luke 24: 36–49;*
     *John 20: 19–29*)
   Luke and John, on the other hand, report that the appearance of Jesus to his eleven disciples did not occur at some unspecified time after Easter day and in Galilee, but took place on the evening of Easter day in Jerusalem, where the disciples had been hiding in a house (Luke 24:36–49; John 20:19–23). So the whole of the Easter events are juxtaposed both in time and space. This is clearly a sign that we are dealing here with a somewhat later phase in the history of the tradition, when the decisive wish was to obtain a narrative context in which the appearance of the angel at the empty tomb to the women is immediately followed by the appearance of Jesus himself to the eleven disciples.
   Both in structure and in individual formulations these two accounts correspond; so that it can be assumed that both evangelists adapted one and the same narrative, handed down to them in tradition. This narrative has two parts. Firstly the appearance as such is depicted. Jesus suddenly steps into their midst and greets them with the *Shalom* blessing: 'Peace be with you!' Then he shows them his hands and his side (John 20:20; Luke 24:39f); by the marks of the nails and the wound in his side (cf. John 19:34) it is intended they should recognize him as the risen Christ. Whereas now the recognition of Jesus, according to John, has the effect that they rejoice (John 20:20),

according to Luke their reaction is that they are startled and terrified. They think they are seeing a ghost (Luke 24:37); and the risen Christ has great difficulty in overcoming their misconception.

His hands and feet are the first proof of the contrary, for 'no ghost has flesh and bones as you can see that I have' (Luke 24:39, NEB). But their disbelief is not yet overcome, however much astonishment and joy they feel. 'They were still unconvinced, still wondering, for it seemed too good to be true' (24:41). So he asks for a piece of fish they have cooked, and eats it before their eyes (v. 42f). Here what we have is not an account of a meal with his disciples, but of a demonstration in their presence intended to open their eyes to recognize the risen Christ.

The same motif of doubt is treated much more laboriously by John. Thomas, who was not present at the appearance of Jesus, got so worked up in his disbelief that he goes so far as to make it a condition: 'unless I see the mark of the nails on his hands, unless I put my finger into the place where the nails were, and my hand into his side, I will not believe it' (John 20:25, NEB). Then Jesus repeats his appearance a week later, in order to convince even this most ardent of all unbelievers that it is really his Master who is facing him. Then Thomas falls at the feet of Jesus: 'My Lord and my God!' (John 20:26–28). Admittedly the evangelist has here added (to this confession by Thomas, that his fundamental disbelief has been removed) the extremely critical response by Jesus: 'Because you have seen me you have found faith. Happy are they who never saw me and yet have found faith' (John 20:29). That is to say: from now on nobody will receive such tangible proof as Thomas in order to assist them to find faith.

In the Church after Easter it will be the case that Jesus's disciples will believe in him without having seen him; and such faith is a prime example of true faith. Similarly, previously, it was not those who saw Jesus performing miracles who were moved to believe in him; it was those who recognized in Jesus

God's emissary, whose 'words are words of eternal life' (John 6:68f), who emerge as the true believers, for in the post-Easter Church, a Christian will not have Jesus visible to him. The mark of true faith will always be the confession of Jesus as the Son of God (John 20:31). Admittedly, according to the evangelist of John's Gospel, faith's criterion is also Jesus of Nazareth in his human manifestation on earth. But in Jesus he sees the Son of God who is one with God his Father (10:30; cf. 14:9f; 17:20) and what he preserves of Jesus are his words (14:21–24) —therefore Jesus's command to Mary Magdalene, forbidding her to fall down before his earthly appearance and forbidding her to touch him, is inserted by the evangelist into the traditional account of Jesus's appearance as it was handed down to him (20:17).

The critical concluding words to Thomas (20:19) point in the same direction. In both passages the evangelist has made a critical interpretation of the tradition as he received it. Whereas, on the one hand, the traditional account was interested in making the point, in as massive and irresistible a manner as possible, that the risen Jesus was really physically Jesus 'in the flesh'; on the other hand John by no means rejected this point as such, but he was intent on correcting the imbalance of the interest being concentrated, in too one-sided a fashion, only on the physical reality of Jesus's manifestation. On the other hand then the evangelist agrees that an essential and indispensable prerequisite of faith in Jesus is belief that in him God's Son has 'come in the flesh' (1 John 4:2f), and that where this is questioned, battle must be waged; for on the fact that 'the word became flesh' (John 1:14; cf. 1 John 1:1–4) depends the possibility that men can hear God's word out of the mouth of his emissary (1:18).

On the other hand, however, the decisive aspect of belief is not his physical incarnation, but his origin in God and his coming from God, his full power and authority from God and his return to God: in short, his one-ness, his unity with God. Thomas confesses Jesus as 'my Lord and my God' and this expresses it correctly—but the truth of it only becomes fully clear, where this faith in Jesus is expressed, and borne witness to, by disciples who have not seen the risen Christ in his physical manifestation.

In the tradition before John, however, the risen Christ appears in order to overcome his disciples' doubts as to his identity and in order to give them proof that he really is physically their Master, the Crucified One. It can be observed how this motif became stronger and stronger as the tradition continued. In Matthew mention of the doubts 'of some' only appears quite marginally. In Luke the proof of identity already dominates the centre of the scene. Finally in John it is expanded into an independent scene which becomes the climax of the entire story of Christ's appearance. For all that, the original motif of mission (Matt. 28:18–20) has not become lost. Both in Luke and in John it has become a second scene. After doubt has been removed, the risen Christ calls his disciples, now convinced in their faith, to their vocation and sends them forth to mission (Luke 24:44–49; John 20:21–33). In structuring this scene, each evangelist gives prominence to a special point of view. In the case of Luke, the prerequisite is that the disciples' eyes should be opened for them to realize that the Old Testament is prophecy of Christ (Luke 24:44f); then they can go forth and proclaim his mission. The risen Christ promises to send the Spirit of God as a mighty aid in their proclamation (Luke 24:49).

Similarly in the case of John also, the sending of the disciples forth to mission (John 20:21) is followed by their being equipped with the power of the Holy Spirit (John 20:22). Their being sent by Jesus corresponds to Jesus being sent by God. The Holy Spirit is not just promised, however, it is given to the disciples on the spot, there and then; and the Holy Spirit serves not only to help them in their proclamation and preaching, but the Holy Spirit fully authorizes them to have valid final jurisdiction over men: 'If you forgive any man's sins, they stand forgiven; if you pronounce them unforgiven,

unforgiven they remain' (John 20:23).

This is not yet (as in Matt. 18:18) in the sense of their responsibility and jurisdiction within the church in matters of church discipline, but is to be understood as the power effective in their preaching enabling them to bring about a decision in their listeners, separating them into believers and non-believers, just as Jesus's words did (cf. John 3:17ff; 5:22ff; 9:39). This too is the original sense of the word to Peter (Matt. 16:16).

### (c)  *The Origin of the Identification Motif (Luke 24: 13–35; John 21: 1–14)*

In the history of the tradition, originally the motif of mission dominates the appearance of Christ as a whole. The motif of proof of identity only comes in subsequently. What are the grounds for the rise and rapid growth of interest in the appearance as such? It is frequently suspected that this development results from theological struggles within the early church. It is reasoned that there were 'gnostic' circles, which had expressed massive doubts as to the physical bodily reality of the appearances of Jesus, and that such doubts were countered by the correspondingly massive reshaping of the stories of his appearances into proofs of the identity of the risen Christ. Yet one must be cautious with such suspicions and conjectures.

The only one passage in the New Testament where such Christological differences are clearly attested, is in the First Letter of John (1 John 4:1ff); and there the conflict is not about the appearance of the risen Christ, but the appearance of Jesus on earth, the incarnation itself, is disputed. Within the stories of his appearance themselves it is only in Luke's Gospel that one could detect what might perhaps be polemical Christological interest.

When the risen Christ expressly emphasizes that he is no ghost, when the disciples thought they were seeing a ghost (Luke 24:39; cf. 24:36), this could be a refutation of an understanding of Jesus's appearance as a disembodied manifestation of a purely spirit being. The anti-gnostic part of the Church, which defended the physical reality of the risen Christ against all other interpretations, would have replied: No, the risen Christ in whom you believe, is not a disembodied spirit-being, but is the Son of God who 'became flesh' (John 1:14). But this interpretation is not certain. A much more obvious solution is to interpret the passage in a similar way to the story of the miraculous appearance of Jesus on the sea of Galilee (Mark 6:45ff). There we are told that Jesus, striding over the sea by night, hastened to the aid of his disciples threatened by the storm: 'but when they saw him walking on the lake, they thought it was a ghost and cried out; for they all saw him and were terrified. But at once he spoke to them: "Take heart! It is I; do not be afraid" ' (Mark 6:49–50).

The disciples' terror, their anxiety lest they were being confronted by a mere phantasm, corresponds to the account in Luke of the disciples' being startled and terrified when Jesus appeared, and their thinking they were 'seeing a ghost' (Luke 24:37). And just as in Mark, the disciples' anxiety is allayed by Jesus himself; so too in Luke's account, the risen Christ has the same objective: 'It is I—do not be afraid'. That is also the sense of what the risen Christ does, when he shows them his hands and his feet and eats a piece of cooked fish.

What the narrator, in both cases, wishes to give sole prominence to, is the reality of the identity of Jesus. In Mark, the disciples' realization that it is Jesus, has the effect that their terror recedes. In Luke, it has the effect that the risen Christ can send the disciples forth to their mission. In both passages the disciples' state of terror is used to bring out the actual fact that really it is Christ himself who appeared; and this highlights the appearance, moving it into the spotlight of the narrative. What we have is thus probably not polemic interest confronting a heretical Christology, but simply a strong positive interest in identifying the risen Christ in his appearance to the disciples with Jesus the teacher and Lord of the disciples, and it is this interest which works itself out in the later phase of the transmission of the accounts of Christ's appearances.

This can be recognized in an especially impressive way in the account of the appearance of Jesus to the two disciples on the way to Emmaus, which Luke has woven into his Easter story (Luke 24:13–35). It is without doubt the most beautiful narrative version of all the Easter stories. However much it is a compact whole, self-contained, rounded off, condensed and lucid, nevertheless it can now be clearly recognized that it grew in several layers. Presumably the earliest nucleus is formed by the meal scene (Luke 24:28–31) to which verses 13 and 15b were the introduction. On the way from Jerusalem to Emmaus two disciples meet Jesus as an unknown traveller. On their arrival in the village they invite him home with them. At the meal they suddenly recognize him from the way he takes the bread, says the blessing, breaks the bread and offers it to them. But hardly have they recognized him when he vanishes from their sight. Now they comprehend why they felt their hearts so on fire as he talked with them on the road (Luke 24:32a). Without a moment's delay they set out and return to Jerusalem, and there give their account of what has happened to them (Luke 24:33a, 35).

In this original form the sudden recognition of Jesus, granted to them at the breaking of the bread, is at the centre. The long journey on foot in company with Jesus as an unrecognized stranger, forms an extremely effective contrast. The recognition is a *re*-recognition: when they see the way the stranger takes over the role of head of the household at the meal the scales fall from their eyes. The stranger is Jesus; he is behaving now with us, as he always used to do in the circle of his disciples! The narrative is only concerned with how this recognition comes to pass. Therefore Jesus vanishes the moment the disciples recognize him. It is all they need, so his vanishing causes them no dismay or regrets. On the contrary they cannot wait to get back to Jerusalem to report the event. The geographical details belong to this early narrative.

It cannot be determined with certainty which place is meant

by the name Emmaus, for there are two places of this name. There is, firstly, present-day 'Amwas, 23 kilometres (or nearly 15 miles) northwest of Jerusalem, which the entire early Church tradition regarded as the Biblical Emmaus. Secondly, there is present-day Colonije, 6 kilometres northwest of Jerusalem. Neither place coincides with the distance mentioned at Luke 24:13. However that does not prove much. Probably the early Church tradition is right.

'Amwas lies between Jerusalem and Lydda: and in Lydda and Joppa there were later Christian communities (Acts 9:32ff). One can assume that the Emmaus story is an old local tradition of the Christian community there. They claimed Jesus's appearance at the meal as the origin of their own community. In this sense the return to Jerusalem also belongs to the old account. The disciples' reporting in the metropolis heightens the importance of the Emmaus Christians. Admittedly, later tradition stressed the primacy of Jerusalem by making quite certain of establishing Christ's appearance to Peter as the *first* appearance, by having the Jerusalem disciples report it to the Emmaus disciples on their return to Jerusalem (cf. 1 Cor. 15:5; Mark 16:7). The early narrative was amplified later, above all by the long conversation on the journey (Luke 24:17-27). Here now the contrast, between the presence of Jesus and the blindness of the two disciples who do not recognize him, is considerably heightened. The disciples are most deeply affected by Jesus's suffering and fate, and they see with his death the collapse of the hope in Jesus as the prophet of the Last Day who will redeem Israel. The events at the empty tomb of Jesus in their view are also part of the catastrophe.

Thereupon Jesus shows them in detail, first of all, that his fate in the Passion corresponds to Old Testament prediction. The opening of their eyes for the messiah prediction in *scripture* (Luke 24:32) thus prepares the opening of their eyes to recognize *Christ himself* (v. 31). From the different concepts with which there is linked the keyword *'opening'* it can be recognized that the conversation during the journey is an interpolation by Luke. In the words of the risen Christ to his eleven disciples (24:44–46) it is a question of 'opening the scriptures'. In the sermons of the apostles, as structured by Luke in Acts (2:22ff; 3:13ff; 10:37ff; 13:23ff), the Passion and Easter story of Jesus is emphasized as the fulfilment of prophetic prediction in 'scripture'. The pre-Lucan narrative on the other hand had its objective in the wonderfully revealed recognition of the identity of the risen Christ with the pre-Easter Lord of the disciples. In this narrative we have before us the original form of the motif, which, in the tradition of the appearance to the eleven disciples, was later grafted on to it.

However, though it is a question of express '*proofs*' of his identity, the Emmaus story is in addition given its special character by a quite simple astounded discerning of the wonderful presence of Jesus at the meal. In just the same manner as he began the communal meal while on earth, he now also begins it as the risen Christ: they recognize him from this habitual procedure. Thus the post-Easter community meal appears as founded by the risen Christ himself. He showed himself as present to his disciples—hence consequently the Christian community knows that it is visited by Christ in its celebration meal. There is a similar atmosphere too about the story of Christ's appearance found in a later appendix to John's Gospel (John 21:1–14). Peter and six other disciples go out fishing on the Lake of Galilee, but fish all night without catching anything. At daybreak they see Jesus standing on the shore but do not recognize him. He calls to them, asking whether they have caught anything. They say they have not. Then he tells them to cast the net out on the right side: and now they make a great catch of fish. The unnamed 'disciple whom Jesus loved' whom we already met, in John, in the story of the tomb, knows that it is Jesus and he tells Peter. Peter plunges into the sea; the others follow in the boat, towing the overfull net. Ashore they find a wood fire with fish cooking on it, and bread. At Jesus's command Peter drags up the net with the freshly caught fish, a hundred and fifty-three fish all told. Now Jesus invites them to have a meal. But nobody dares to ask him who he is, for they all know. Jesus takes the bread and hands it to them, and likewise gives them the fish. This story is late in literary terms: in terms of the history of the tradition, on the other hand, it shows in a very interesting way, a growing together of motifs from earlier and later tradition.

If one considers verses 1–14 on their own, the story shows a certain similarity with the Emmaus story. At the centre is the recognition of Jesus, who first of all was unrecognized when he appeared. Yet this recognition takes place in different phases, so to speak. The first to know is 'the disciple whom Jesus loved'; through him Peter learns it; and at the meal on the shore all of them know—but it is and remains a knowing surrounded by secrecy, knowledge that does not bring release and joy but dejection and anguish. It is only in the following scene that Jesus breaks the spell, by asking Peter thrice 'Do you love me?', and three times then commands Peter to tend and feed his sheep (John 21:15ff). The author who composed this supplementary chapter thus wishes to have the whole preceding story of Christ's appearance understood as being only an introduction to this dialogue with Peter. If one then looks more closely at the story in verses 1–14, one sees that two motifs stand side by side, but not quite balanced against each other. On the one hand, there is firstly the wonderful catch of fish following Jesus's word of advice, which initiates the occasion of the recognition. Peter here stands out from the other disciples: they have gone out fishing at night on his initiative (v. 3); he plunges into the water in order to be the first to reach Jesus (v. 7); and alone he pulls the overfull net ashore (v. 11). On the other hand, there is then mention of a meal, which Jesus has already prepared for his disciples, and to which he calls them. They do not dare to ask who he is, because they know. He opens the meal, however, by taking the bread and handing it on to them (v. 12f).

So far as the story of the fish catch is concerned, the similarity

with Luke's story of Peter's calling is striking (Luke 5:1–11).
It also takes place on the shore of the sea of Galilee. Here, too,
Jesus challenges Peter to cast out his net, although Peter argues
that they have caught nothing all night; and following Jesus's
instruction they catch an almost too-abundant haul. Then
Peter falls at the feet of Jesus, who calls the fisherman to follow
him and, in future, be a fisher of men. Corresponding to this
we have, in John 21, the thrice-repeated call to Peter to be the
shepherd of Jesus's sheep (vv. 15, 16, 17). So, if one reads the
narrative of the wonderful catch of fish (vv. 1–8) as the introduction to the following calling of Peter (v. 15ff), we then have
a narrative context which corresponds to the story in Luke 5.
Possibly the strange detail, quoted at John 21:11, that Peter
pulled ashore the net with 153 fish all by himself, is to be
explained as an allusion encoded in cipher referring to his
special function among the remaining disciples (cf., similarly,
the number 666 in Rev. 13:18) then this would correspond
to the word about the fisher of men at Luke 5:10. All this
strengthens the suspicion that both narratives go back to one
and the same original story of Peter's calling.

    This leads to the question whether this original story on
which they were based, told of a pre-Easter calling to vocation
as in Luke 5, or whether, as at John 21, it told of the call to
vocation as happening at Easter. Probably the latter is the case.
This probability is indicated by a comparison between Luke
5:1–11 and Mark 1:16–20. Here there is an account of two
pairs of brothers receiving the call; Peter is called together with
his brother Andrew. Luke linked this story very skilfully
with the Peter story, though admittedly so that the three others
from Mark 1 are only named as companions of Peter (Luke
5:10); but the calling to be fishers of men, according to
Mark 1:17, applies to both Peter and Andrew; whereas,
according to Luke 5, Peter alone receives the call. There are
thus two different competing traditions. The account in
Mark 1 tells of a call to vocation before Easter; Luke 5, on the
other hand, probably originally had the vocation occurring at

Easter, since it only had available the parallel accounts not only in John 21 but in all early testimonies telling of the calling of Peter by the risen Christ. From this it can be recognized as a relatively old narrative version of the formulaic tradition transmitted in 1 Cor. 15:5 where we had an account of the call of Peter corresponding to that of the twelve or eleven disciples at Matthew 28:16–20. The account of the call to vocation is now, at John 21, the framework, into which is inserted a story of an appearance of Jesus of another kind, the story telling of the wonderful recognizing of Jesus, which occurred to a group of seven disciples (John 21:2) in the context of a meal (21:12f). In its objective and its atmosphere this story is similar to the pre-Easter appearance story at Mark 6:45–52, the story which was already brought in for comparison above.

During their nocturnal battle with the waters of the sea of Galilee which had been whipped up by a storm the disciples see Jesus coming towards them, walking on the water. They cry out in terror, thinking he is a ghost and even after he has spoken to them and said to them who he is, they are still terrified. It is the manifestation as such, which evokes the response which was widespread throughout the entire ancient world, namely, the experience of terror and oppressive uneasy awe at the proximity of something numinous. So there remains in John 21, too, an atmosphere of uneasy anxiety, which is triggered off by the very knowledge of who he is.

Among the Easter stories the only comparison remaining to be made is with the Emmaus narrative. On both occasions the situation of a meal plays a role. On both occasions the motif of the wonderful recognition of the risen Christ determines the nature and sequence of the plot or action. It could have been these stories of appearances (recognition narratives) which were the cause of the subsequent expansion of the stories at Luke 24:36ff and John 20:19ff. The motif shaping the narrative altered from a motif stressing the *experiencing* of the risen Christ, to a motif stressing the *proof* of the identity. John 21 is an example, after all, of the coalescing of the motif of the call to vocation and the motif of the wonderful experiencing of Christ's identity. The step from this to the superimposition of the proof of identity on top of the call to vocation (Luke 24, John 20) is not a large step.

### (d)  *A Later Catalogue of Appearances (Mark 16:9–20)*

It remains to cast a glance over the final section of Mark which was added later (Mark 16:9–20). In the early manuscripts, preferred on grounds of textual criticism, this section is lacking and is only found in the mass of later manuscripts. Thus the unanimously held verdict that we are here dealing with an addition to the text of Mark's Gospel, from a very much later period, (from as late, possibly, as the third century), would appear to be compellingly cogent and conclusive. To be sure, this does not mean that that part was itself only formed at this late period. Very probably it came into existence as early as the second century in Church tradition, with the concern of bringing together all the traditions in circulation about appearances of the risen Christ.

Such catalogue-like compilations existed at a very early period, as the list at 1 Cor. 15:5–7 proves. The section at Mark 16:9ff is of a similar character. One after another there are enumerated:

1. an appearance to Mary Magdalene; she informs her companions of what has befallen her, but they do not believe her (vv. 9–11; cf. John 20:1f, 18; Luke 24:9–11);
2. an appearance to two disciples on the way to a village, who also make the remaining report but encounter disbelief (v. 12f; cf. Luke 24:13–35);
3. the final appearance to the eleven disciples, when Jesus initially scolds them for their persistent unbelief (v. 14) and then goes on to set them their task to go forth on mission to preach to 'the whole of creation' and baptize believers and he promises them the wonderful gift of tongues, the power of healing and healthy physical

resistance (Mark 16:15–18). After talking with them thus Jesus is taken up into heaven (v. 19); thereafter the disciples go out to make their proclamation everywhere and accomplish their missionary task with worldwide success (v. 20).

The arrangement of the whole section corresponds to the structure of the pre-Lucan and pre-John story of Christ's appearance with its division into two parts:

1. the overcoming of disbelieving doubt and
2. the missionary task (Luke 24:36ff; John 20:19ff).

Under the heading of the first motif, the appearance to Mary Magdalene, and the appearance to the two disciples, are both arranged together, as a preliminary structure leading into the effect of their accounts which in both cases encounter withering doubts on the part of the eleven disciples. Unmistakably nevertheless the main emphasis is laid on the missionary task they are given. It can be seen how powerfully this original *N.B* motif of the appearances of the risen Christ persists in tradition right through to that late period.

### (e) *Synopsis*

Let us summarize the results of our examination of the accounts of Christ's appearances. At the earliest stage in the transmission of the tradition, previous to Paul and contemporary with Paul, the appearances of Jesus are recorded in short formulaic sentences. They express the missionary credentials and the full powers and authority conferred on specifically named Christians, whom the risen Christ in his heavenly power and glory has called to be his special instruments. In this sense, Christ's appearances to Peter, James and Paul, were reported in the whole of primitive Christianity only in this short form, in which only the bare fact is mentioned. There were not complete stories. Accordingly Mark did not tell the story of the decisive first appearance to Peter and the

Twelve (1 Cor. 15:5), which he added to the Easter story as it was handed down to him, but only drew attention to it with his reference at Mark 16:7.

Before Mark, the two traditions were different in nature and distinctly separate. Firstly, there was the Easter story at the empty tomb, forming the concluding section of the old account of the Passion. Secondly, there were the short formulae, incorporating a record of appearances of the heavenly Lord, legitimizing the call to vocation of certain leaders with authority in the sphere of primitive Christian mission.

Yet already Paul quoted the traditions of the appearances of the risen Christ as an argument in support of the proclamation of the resurrection, when it was a question of Paul combating the criticisms circulating in his Christian community in Corinth with regard to his proclaimed hope of the resurrection of the dead at the end of time (1 Cor. 15). Paul's composition of a formula including basic data of the story of the Passion of Jesus (his death, burial and resurrection, together with both the first appearances to Peter and the Twelve (1 Cor. 15:3–5) and expanded by mention of further appearances (1 Cor. 15:6–7) ) also shows an already widespread tendency at an early period to incorporate the separately transmitted traditions of Christ's appearances into the story of Jesus's Passion and the Easter story.

Mark is a further early representative of this tendency. He found in Matthew a successor, who, for the first time in one narrative context, forged a link between the events at the tomb and the appearance in Galilee to the Eleven. Alongside this story another narrative took shape dealing with the same appearance to the disciples, and Luke and John made use of this. The story is set in Jerusalem, on the evening of Easter Day itself; in other words, prominence is being given to establishing the same context in time and place, for both the proclamation of the resurrection by the angel at the empty tomb and the appearance of the risen Christ to his disciples. In establishing this connection both Matthew and John give a linking intermediate role to Jesus's appearance to the women who discovered the empty tomb. An alteration in content can also be detected here: whereas, originally, the appearance of the risen Christ was in order to call the disciples to their vocation of mission; now the motif, of Christ proving his identity in order to overcome the persistent doubts of the disciples, moves into the foreground. This motif is to be found in its most unsubtly direct form in the story of doubting Thomas, at John 20:24ff.

In the Emmaus story (Luke 24:13–35) we can trace the motif back to its origin. The story is concerned with the wonderful gift of recognition of Jesus at the meal, after he had been unrecognized at first when he appeared. Tradition recounted this appearance in order to record the origin of the local Christian community in Emmaus. A story of a similar character is the one, adapted and worked into the supplementary chapter at the end of John's Gospel, telling of a meal the disciples have with Jesus at which he reveals his identity to them (John 21:9ff). For all that, the original motif of the call to vocation by the risen Christ has been preserved up to the latest phase in the transmission of tradition (Mark 16:15ff; John 21:15ff). The original conception of the appearance is that the risen Christ in his heavenly power and glory becomes visible to those whom he wishes to call to vocation. This is how Paul experienced it (Gal. 1:15f), and we can visualize the experience of the witnesses before him as corresponding to this conception too.

It is against the background of this underlying conception that we must view the fact that neither in Mark nor Matthew nor John is there to be found any remark concerning whence Jesus came at his appearance, or where he went afterwards. For the Christians of the entire early period that was no problem. For them the risen Christ is in heaven with God; and whenever he appears as the risen Christ then obviously he comes from heaven and returns thence. Since, however, there is nowhere any mention of a return to heaven, we can more probably assume that those who received these appearances of the risen Christ saw him in his heavenly glory. It is in this sense, at any rate, that Paul's formulation, at Gal. 1:16, is to be understood, when it speaks of God having given him a 'revelation' of his Son in order that he might proclaim him among the heathen.

The word 'revelation' has a fixed meaning in Judaic apocalyptic tradition. The word 'revelation' is a designation for wonderful experiences happening to individual distinguished men, to whom through God, or mostly through an angel, facts and circumstances known only in heaven, or future happenings, are 'revealed' as 'secrets'. A good example of this is the description of the Seer in Revelation who describes the visions granted to him thus: 'I, John, was on the island called Patmos . . .; It was on the Lord's Day; and I was caught up by the Spirit; and behind me I heard a loud voice, like the sound of a trumpet, which said to me: "Write down what you see in a book" (RSV "book", NEB "scroll") . . . I turned to see whose voice it was that spoke to me; and when I turned I saw seven standing lamps of gold, and among the lamps one like a Son of Man . . .' (Rev. 1:9ff). The son of man whom he sees, is the risen Christ ruling from God's throne in heaven (1:17f). He even sees him later at the moment when, having arisen from the dead, he steps before God's throne (Rev. 5:1ff). Correspondingly, the martyr Stephen, according to the account in Acts, sees 'the heavens opened, and the Son of Man standing at the right hand of God' (Acts 7:5b, RSV).

And in the same way as the Seer, in the Revelation of John, receives the command from the risen Christ in heaven to write down what is shown to him in heaven, so too this is the conception we must have of the way in which Paul and the witnesses before him experienced the call to mission from heaven (cf. Gal. 1:11f). So it makes no fundamental difference whether Paul learns of his task from heaven as the Seer in Revelation, or whether the stories of the appearances in Matthew and John have the risen Christ appearing on earth. In both cases the crucial point is that it is the Heavenly Lord who appears. Therefore there is no problem about where he comes from and goes to. The risen Christ appears suddenly—for example through locked doors (John 20:19), and disappears in the same manner (cf. e.g. Luke 24:31). Mostly nothing at all is said about his whereabouts. Matthew's account concludes with the final words of Jesus to his disciples: 'I am with you always, to the end of time' (Matt. 28:20). Likewise John ends with the words of the risen Christ to Thomas (John 20:29): 'Happy are they who never saw me and yet have found faith' (NEB); 'Blessed are those who have not seen and yet believe' (RSV).

The entire New Testament tradition knows nothing of Jesus's Ascension after his appearances, for to them the risen Christ is already in heaven before he appears, or he appears during his Ascension (John 20:17). The only exceptions are the writings of Luke. Therefore we must briefly turn to them in the following section.

(f) *Account of the Ascension*

Firstly, it must be remembered that faith in Jesus as the Lord raised on high, who sits in heaven on the right hand of God and is Lord over all powers, formed part of the faith in the risen Christ right from the beginning throughout the whole extent of primitive Christianity. Christ's being raised from the dead and his being lifted up on high belong together (Rom. 8:34; Eph. 1:19ff; Col. 1:18ff; Hebr. 1:3; 13:20f). Indeed mention is often only made of Jesus being raised on high, while the resurrection is silently taken for granted (e.g. Phil. 2:9–11; Hebr. 1:3; 5:5ff; John 16:28). That the crucified Christ has come to life, is, when seen from this point of view, only one element in the context of his triumphant ascent and his entering into power at the side of God.

What we have exclusively in Luke and in Acts, is not belief in Christ raised on high, but rather a description of his ascent as a special occurrence after his resurrection, and as a conclusion to the period of his earthly appearances. The two accounts

diverge from one another to a considerable degree. At the end
of Luke's Gospel the following is related: after Jesus had ended
his address to his disciples sending them out into the world,
'he led them out as far as Bethany, and blessed them with
uplifted hands; and in the act of blessing he parted from them
(and was carried up into heaven). And they returned to
Jerusalem with great joy, and spent all their time in the temple
praising God' (Luke 24:50–53).

In some manuscripts the phrase (in parentheses above)
about his Ascension is lacking, so that the text speaks only of
Jesus parting from them. This however is probably a subsequent deletion, intended to balance the end of Luke's Gospel
and the introduction to Acts, where there is once again a
report of Jesus's Ascension (Acts 1:9f). This duplication is,
however, probably an intentional stylistic device on the part of
Luke, showing the connection between the story of Jesus and
the following account of mission, and, by the repetition,
making the connection more eye-catching. In Luke 24, the
Ascension is depicted as Jesus's final leavetaking from his
disciples on earth. Therefore Christ blesses them: in the Bible
stories of fathers, the patriarch blesses his sons before he dies.
There is the well known story of Jacob who deviously obtains
by fraud from the dying patriarch the blessing which by right
Esau the elder son should have received (Gen. 27). Likewise
Jacob blesses the sons of his son Joseph before he dies (Gen. 48).
But above all Moses, before his death, blesses the Israelites
(Deut. 33). Correspondingly, King Solomon blesses the whole
assembly at the great divine service of consecration of the
temple, before the people return to their towns and villages
(1 Kings 8:54ff; cf. Ecclesiasticus 50:20f; and Jos. 22:6f). The
raised arms are the gesture of blessing as a symbol that is the
blessing of God which the person pronouncing the blessing is
wishing down from heaven (cf. Numbers 6:22ff). Finally, in
the Apocryphal Book Tobit, the archangel Raphael blesses the
father Tobit and his Son Tobias before once again ascending to
heaven (Tob. 12:16ff). These are enough examples to show the

sense of Jesus's act of blessing: Christ ascending gives his people into God's saving care which comes down to them from heaven.

The account of the Ascension at the introduction of Acts is differently constructed. Here Luke once again gives a flashback to the final scene of the Gospel where the risen Christ has revealed himself to his disciples, by many proofs, as living, and has instructed them to remain in Jerusalem in order to receive the Holy Spirit, as promised, as a gift from heaven (Acts 1:4f). The disciples' question, whether he is now going to go on as Messiah to establish for Israel the promised kingdom of the end of time (1:6), is cut short by his answer that it is not a question for the time being of the beginning of the end of time, but it is a matter of enabling the disciples through the Spirit of God to carry the proclamation from Jerusalem out 'to the ends of the earth' (1:8). The time now beginning is the time of World Mission.

Thus Luke firmly places the original motif from the traditions about Christ's appearances with great emphasis right in the centre of the scene. Next follows the Ascension: 'When he had said that, as they watched, he was lifted up, and a cloud removed him from their sight. As he was going, and as they were gazing intently into the sky, all at once there stood beside them two men in white (cf. Luke 24:4) who said, "Men of Galilee, why stand there looking up into the sky? This Jesus, who has been taken away from you up to heaven, will come in the same way as you have seen him go" ' (Acts 1:9–11). Then they returned from Mount Olivet to Jerusalem (v. 12).

Luke does everything here in order to turn the attention of his readers, as with the disciples, away from Jesus's Ascension and to focus it on the story now beginning of the mission on earth; a story which he goes on to describe in the following section with great artistic skill and breathtaking theological élan.

Why does he wish to deflect the disciples' and reader's attention? These two angels give us the answer: because Christ's Ascension on a cloud has no other significance than to

bring Jesus to the place from which he will return at the end.
That is, Jesus's leavetaking has its appropriate time; it serves
firstly as a caesura between the story of Jesus and the story of
mission following it. The disciples now ought to concentrate
entirely on their mission; for it is their task to proclaim the
story of Jesus over all the earth so that on his return at the end
of time he will find a body of disciples drawn from all the
peoples of the world.

As can be seen, that is a theological 'programme' of great
power. According to Luke one should not think of the coming
of the end of time, without thinking of it as an incentive
spurring on to maximum missionary activity. For the end of
time with Jesus's second coming is bound up with the worldwide success of the mission to all peoples (cf. already Mark
13:10). So Jesus's Ascension is here resolutely subordinated to
the motif of the sending forth to mission which stands at the
centre of the traditions of Christ's appearances. From this it
can be concluded that Luke knows of the Ascension from
tradition. He arranges it, inserting it into his story of Easter:
Ascension ends the time during which Christ makes his
appearances. Forty days is the time this lasted, according to
Acts 1:3. That is naturally not meant in the sense of a
historically correct specific chronological measurement. Forty
is a Biblical number (cf. Ps. 95:10 about Israel's time in the
wilderness; 1 Kings 19:8 about the Prophet Elijah's length of
fast). Luke is only concerned with indicating it was a limited
length of time (cf. Acts 13:31). Why? For him it is essential
that the eleven disciples, as the later apostles of the Church, are
able to testify as eye-witnesses to the story of Jesus right from
the beginning and, especially, bear witness to his presence after
his resurrection (cf. Acts 2:32; 3:15; 5:32; 10:40–42).

Precisely this is the alteration in content, in the conception of
the appearances of Jesus, which we find in Luke: Jesus does not
appear from heaven, but shows himself to those who are later
to be witnesses, on earth, as proof that he, the crucified Christ is
really living. 'Why search among the dead for one who lives?'

the angel significantly remarks to the women at the tomb (Luke 24:5; cf. 24:23).

And in the later preaching of the apostles it is one of the most decisive central sentences, that God did not leave his Messiah in death but snatched him away from death (Acts 2:24ff; 13:34f; 17:31–32); indeed, Luke can go so far as to characterize the apostolic preaching thus: it is concerned with 'proclaiming in Jesus the resurrection from the dead' (Acts 4:2, RSV; cf. Acts 23:6ff). So we recognize a theologically reflected development of the motif which, in the later phase of the transmission of the traditions of stories of Christ's appearances, pushed itself into a central position, namely, the motif of the proof of identity. Already in the story of Christ's appearance, told at Luke 24:36ff, Luke has structured it to bring out the fact that the person appearing is really Jesus in the flesh. Now it can be seen why that is so important to him: on the physical reality of Christ's appearance in the flesh depends the reality of God's act of raising Jesus from the dead, and this reality of being raised from the dead is something which Christians can themselves hope for.

Paul the theologian champions the physical reality of the resurrection with the same commitment with which he insists to his Corinthians on the reality of future resurrection of the dead (1 Cor. 15:12ff). From this aspect of Paul's interest, Jesus's appearances are valid proofs of his resurrection (Acts 1:3). Accordingly they have their earthly timing just as do all phases of his story. According to Luke the risen Christ has his place not in heaven but still on earth. So Luke virtually required the Ascension tradition: through it the risen Christ was taken-up from his earthly sojourn with his disciples into heaven to God. But it is not the removal to heaven as such which interests the theologian Luke: it is the earthly mission in which the happenings are a continuation of Jesus's story, going on until at some time he will once again return from heaven to earth.

Now Luke no doubt did not simply invent these new

thoughts himself. He only thought out the theological implica-
tions of the tendencies in the tradition as he found it. So the
resurrection must have been spoken of, as marking the end of
Jesus's earthly sojourn, already before Luke. The late Mark-
ending is a good example of this. Here, after the risen Christ
has informed the disciples of their missionary task, it is
reported: 'So after talking with them the Lord Jesus was taken
up into heaven, and he took his seat at the right hand of God'
(Mark 16:19). The phrase, about the Lord Jesus being taken
up into heaven, is taken over verbally from the Old Testament
story (2 Kings 2:11) of Elijah being 'carried up to heaven'.
And Psalm 110:1 talks of 'sitting at the right hand of God'—
a passage, by the way, which in primitive Christianity was
always regarded as testimony to Jesus being raised up on high,
and was frequently used.

Here one sees how the Ascension story arose: what was
handed down was the primitive Christian article of faith about
Jesus being raised and seated at the right hand of God. In the
earlier period it was seen as referring to Jesus's resurrection.
When, however, Jesus's resurrection was later celebrated as the
first great divine miracle of raising from the dead, and where
Christ's appearances are understood as the risen Christ proving
that he is himself back to earth, then Christ's being taken up
into heaven had to be reported as a special act and one
separate from the resurrection. As a model there was the Old
Testament story of Elijah being taken up before the very eyes of
his pupil Elisha. The story at Acts 1:10 is also inspired by this
Old Testament narrative. Probably the connection between
Jesus's Ascension and the disciples' receiving the Holy Spirit
(Acts 1:4f.8; 2:1ff) is also derived from the Story of Elijah,
where, namely, we learn that Elisha previously requested his
teacher that, after his departure, he might let him inherit a
share of his spirit (2 Kings 2:9f); and, indeed, after Elijah had
been taken, Elisha had his wish fulfilled (2 Kings 2:15).

In an entirely different context in tradition, incidentally,
Jesus, in John's Gospel, says, in what is virtually a doctrinal

utterance, 'If I do not go, your Advocate [i.e. the Spirit of God] will not come, whereas if I go, I will send him to you.' (John 16:7). Whereas, however, John regarded Jesus's resurrection and Ascension as one single nexus of events, between which Christ's appearances were intervening events in which the risen Christ, so to speak, on the way past as he was ascending to heaven, identified himself to his followers (cf. John 20:17); and whereas, even in the catalogue of Christ's appearances, in the conclusion added to Mark, there still predominates the idea that all the appearances took place one after another on the same Easter day, Luke alone is interested in making a clear distinction between the resurrection and the Ascension and an intervening period of forty days during which the risen Christ is present with his disciples.

Acts stands alone with this arrangement, in the choir of many voices chanting the tradition of primitive Christianity. Even Luke adheres to the generally held view of Jesus's Ascension, marking the end of his appearances, as taking place on Easter Day itself. It was only when the four Gospels and Acts were incorporated into one canon of the Early Church that the need arose to fit all the Easter events recorded in the New Testament into one harmonized and synchronized chronological order. And Acts, going furthest with the broad scope of its conception, marked the framework within which the Gospel accounts had to fit. In the Church's liturgical order it is only since the fourth century that we have evidence of a separate Feast of the Ascension forty days after Easter.

## Chapter Two

# Significance of the Concept of the Resurrection

When one considers how difficult at the present day it is for people to understand each other, and how mutual understanding requires concentrated effort and single-minded interest, then it is clear that the most difficult task in comprehension which we can set ourselves is going to be to understand what was said in bygone times when it is only available in written form. For texts cannot be questioned like present-day partners in a conversation, and asked about their opinions, their interpretations or the meaning of what they say. Texts are rigidly solidified language. Anyone wishing to understand texts must find his way into the past movement of language, must try to go through this development again re-visualizing it as it was originally viewed. Probably one can do this only by bringing it into the present. Anyone wishing to understand texts of bygone periods properly has to go a stage further and trace the thorny, difficult, strenuous path leading from a remoter past to the stage which is contemporary with the texts but which is still the past for us.

For the first century Christians a great deal was self-evident, which is no longer self-explanatory for us. What is self-evident is naturally never expressly stated, it is inherent in the concrete situation but even more so it is present in the connotations, overtones and many layers of experience implicit in the contexts, embodied in each and every language. Words do already have a meaning when they are used here and now. Pictures, associations, ideas, concepts, thoughts, which are triggered as we speak, already have a previous history, which is the pre-condition on which we make our claim on them, and which is necessary in order that we can be understood by our

74

partners. In short, language presupposes tradition. It is only because we live in tradition that we can speak. But tradition, which is present and effective in spoken language, does not show itself: it is, mostly, the indeterminate medium of language in which both the speaker and the person addressed usually share. Therefore the more successful one is in comprehending the *tradition* in which, so to speak, the language of a text is at home, then the clearer and more certain will be one's comprehension of the *text itself*.

When, therefore, we seek to comprehend the message conveyed by the testimony of the earliest Christians about Jesus's resurrection, in order to see what they are trying to say, we must try to illuminate the contexts of motifs, conceptual contexts, the thought patterns and connotations, all the various contexts in which they spoke about the resurrection. Now, since the earliest Christians were mostly Jews before they became Christians, we can begin by assuming that the Jewish tradition was by and large their natural apperception, the mental sphere in which they understood their Christian faith and the linguistic framework for their expression of their faith. Accordingly, in the following section, we will turn to the Jewish concepts of resurrection, in the expectation of obtaining, as it were, an interpreter for the statements made about resurrection by the earliest Christians.

This naturally cannot mean that one can trace straight direct linear descent as if Christianity were purely derivative, as if nothing new, nothing unique of its own, nothing special was introduced with Christianity. Comparison with Judaistic texts will, on the contrary, bring out all the more clearly the specifically Christian content. It is only important to reject the notion of Christianity as falling from heaven, into the midst of the history of religion in antiquity, devoid of any historical context or preconditions, into a sort of vacuum designed to preserve the absolute unconditional truth of the Christian content matter, the Christian 'cause'.

What is absolute does not manifest itself in history by being

incomparably original. What is historically new reveals itself as
superior to the old source out of which it grows by being more
powerfully convincing. Accordingly, comprehension of what is
new has to begin with what preceded it. In this chapter we will
examine what existed beforehand; and then in the final
chapter we will attempt to understand what is new, what is
specifically Christian, in the New Testament resurrection
message as such, and reflect on it.


1. LIFE AND DEATH IN THE OLD TESTAMENT

(a) *Life and Death*

Important and central as the theme of the resurrection may
be in the New Testament, in the Old Testament it is only to be
found completely on the periphery. For the Israelites of all the
early centuries up to and into the second century before Christ,
all religious interest was concentrated on life between birth and
death. The natural death of a person who has grown old is the
natural end of life, which fundamentally has its own appointed
time. Whoever dies with Abraham 'at a good old age, after a
very long life' (Gen. 25:8, NEB) or, (as the RSV puts it), 'in a
good old age, an old man and full of years', is a person whose
life has become full upon death. Thought of *death* only causes a
person to take *life* seriously in a final sense (Ps. 90:12). ('Teach
us to order our days rightly, that we may enter the gate of
wisdom.') Only sudden premature death is to be feared. It is
such death which is the subject of a death lamentation dirge
(cf. 2 Sam. 1:17ff; 3:33f). The sick person or person in danger
prays to God to be saved from death, and when the danger has
been survived he praises the Saviour of his life—as in Psalm 116:
'The sorrows of death compassed me, and the pains of hell got
hold upon me: I found trouble and sorrow. Then called I upon
the name of the Lord, O Lord, I beseech thee deliver, my
soul. . . .' 'For thou hast delivered my soul from death, mine
eyes from tears, and my feet from falling. I will walk before the
Lord in the land of the living' (Ps. 116:3f, 8f, AV).

These sentences which in the New Testament are regarded as a prediction of Jesus's resurrection (Acts 2:24ff), were originally meant in a non-otherwordly sense. Everyday earthly life is the place for man, and at the same time God's place. 'The dead praise not the Lord, neither any that go down into silence. But we will bless the Lord from this time forth and for evermore' (Ps. 115:17f, AV). 'Turn, O Lord, save my life; . . . For in death there is no remembrance of thee; in Sheol who can give thee praise?' (Ps. 6:4–5, RSV). This is expressed drastically in the story of the illness and death of David's child which was born of his adultery with Uriah's wife: David eats no food for days, and, dressed in mourning, prays day and night for the child's life. But when news of the child's death reaches him he breaks off his lamentation, washes, puts on fresh clothes, prays in the temple and breaks his fast. To his servants he answers: 'While the boy was still alive I fasted and wept, thinking, it may be that the Lord will be gracious to me, and the boy may live. But now that he is dead, why should I fast? Can I bring him back again? I shall go to him; he will not come back to me.' (2 Sam. 12:22f).

The God of Israel is a God of the living (Mark 12:27). The covenant which he has made with his chosen people is based on a mutual inviolable promise by both partners. Israel all its days is to allow its life to be determined by obedience to the will of its God; in return for this God promises Israel protection and furtherance of its life. God's part in the Covenant is to save Israel from its foes and bless its daily life; God's human partners' contribution is their obedience and brotherly love. And so the Israelites experience this goodness, which is immediate, all-encompassing, all-permeating goodness, in their lives as a gift of their God: 'If you will obey the Lord your God by diligently observing all his commandments which I lay upon you this day, then the Lord your God will raise you high above all nations of the earth, and all these blessings shall come upon you and light upon you, because you obey the Lord your God' (Deut. 28:1f, NEB). So runs the introduction to a long

final passage in God's laws delivered by Moses. Here blessings
are promised to those who are obedient; and curses are
intimated to those who are disobedient. But anyone of the
opinion that this passage might be dealing with blessings and
curses referring to the heavenly Beyond, should look at the
crass, glaring this-worldliness of the descriptions of the blessings
and curses: 'A blessing on you in the city; a blessing on you in
the country. A blessing on the fruit of your body, the fruit of
your land and of your cattle, the offspring of your herds and
of your lambing flocks. A blessing on your basket and your
kneading-trough' (Deut. 28:3–5), and so it continues in a
lengthy series. Israel's proverbial 'wisdom', the teaching drawn
from experience tested and proven throughout generations and
submitted to Israel's youth to be tested in future experience,
comments on the latter solemn proclamation as the fruit of
obedience in faith: 'Righteousness exalts a nation, but sin is a
reproach to any people' (Prov. 14:34, RSV). 'The fear of the
Lord prolongs life, but the years of the wicked will be short'
(Prov. 10:27, RSV). Indeed we even read: 'I have been young,
and now am old; yet I have not seen the righteous forsaken or
his children begging bread' (Ps. 37:25, RSV).

## (b) *'Doing' and 'Faring'*

It is wrong to see all these sentences, which we have quoted
and which could easily be multiplied, in an isolated sense as
'religious' statements in some way distinct from everyday
reality and experience. On the contrary religion is entirely
experience here, and the reality of everyday experience is
absolutely religious. A basic principle of reflection about
human activity and experience of the human lot is expressed at
Proverbs 26:27: 'He who digs a pit will fall into it, and a stone
will come back upon him who starts it rolling.' What this
proverbial guiding principle implies is that there is a causal
link between what a person *does* and what he then *experiences* as
his lot. Evil deeds reap a bad fate, good deeds reap a good fate.
And only when the doing has found its equivalent in how the

doer fares, only then is the activity 'full'.

Therefore Abraham the Just, dies with a 'full' life: his life has corresponded to his deeds; Abraham has, so to speak, reaped his just rewards: death does not break off something incomplete, it only rounds it off and completes it. Since the life of the Israelites, as we have said, is determined so completely beyond question by their relationship with God, then the Israelites too also participate in this law of the correspondence between 'doing' and 'faring'. As it says at Proverbs 29:6, RSV, 'An evil man is ensnared in his transgression, but a righteous man sings and rejoices.' Sin is all a person's activity against God's will; justice is all activity in which for his part a person conforms to the correct relationship with God. Sin—so the saying indicates —brings disaster with it; for sinful activity breaks the whole intact saving relationship with God; the salvation, which God has promised to his partner cannot be given to a sinner. Doing what is just and righteous, however, brings with it salvation for in the covenant with God it is intended that justice and salvation shall correspond, on the part of both partners. Salvation is sent by God to the Just. It is only the just person who experiences salvation. It is no contradiction in Jewish thought that a person thus works out his own fate by his own doing; and yet his fate comes from God's hand. The relationship with God is so fundamentally based on activity, that for God, as well as for man, contemporary reality is understood as the result of past doing: man acts and God sends him the corresponding experience to be undergone.

Since salvation, in the sense of complete fulfilment of life on earth, is fundamentally only dispensed by God, and, since God has only promised salvation to those who are just and righteous, then God's activity and human activity are balanced, corresponding in the same way as a person's doings, and his experience of the subsequent result and effects are bound together. This explains the much disputed sentence of Paul's which is thus shown to be in keeping with Jewish thinking: 'You must work out your own salvation in fear and trembling;

for it is God who works in you, inspiring both the will and the deed, for his own chosen purpose' (Phil. 2:13, NEB).

### (c)  *Adverse Experiences*

Now there were certainly in Israel, frequently, isolated experiences which contradicted this fundamental principle. Not all misfortune could be recognized as corresponding to preceding wrongdoing; and above all much irreproachable just-dealing and righteousness awaited in vain to reap its good harvest. Job, who though a just man yet had to undergo an excessive amount of illness and suffering, remains a theological riddle. And in Ecclesiastes, the book of the 'preacher' Solomon, there can be found an abundance of examples of moving resignation regarding the question of theodicy. But, as a whole, early Israel never doubted, far less gave up, the principle of the accord between life and religion.

It is against this background that that exciting confrontation between the people of Israel and the prophets has to be understood. Men like Amos and Hosea recognized that Israel's behaviour was completely and beyond any doubt sinful and that, accordingly, total breakdown in the relationship with God was the inevitable consequence. So the prophets strike, with their predictions of damnation in the name of God, right into the midst of the general self-righteous and complacent piety of the self-satisfied people, which is blind and does not recognize its behaviour as sin, and draw the appropriate consequences, namely, that they must change their ways radically before the catastrophe of God's anger befalls them. Certainly when people are in political distress they begin to lament to God, confess their guilt and beg for forgiveness. Hosea hears them saying to one another: 'Come, let us return to the Lord for he has torn us and will heal us, he has struck us and he will bind up our wounds; after two days he will revive us, on the third day he will restore us, that in his presence we may live. Let us humble ourselves, let us strive to know the Lord (whose justice dawns like the morning light), and its dawning is as sure as the sunrise. It will come to us like a shower, like spring rains that water the earth' (Hos. 6: 1–3, NEB).

In this liturgy, placed by the prophet on the lips of his generation, there lies bitter irony. The prophet lets their so unquestioningly held faith in the goodness of God, who will overlook Israel's transgression, always quickly take pity on his chosen people again, not leave them, nor abandon them to their foes, he lets this faith just as unquestioningly shade imperceptibly into the Canaanite nature religion surrounding Israel. In the Canaanite religion the cyclical succession of fruit and harvest, rain and drought, growth, ripening, withering and new growth were seen as a mythical primitive happening, which concerns the Godhead itself. At regularly recurring intervals the divinity itself dies for two days and comes alive again on the third day. The history of religion in antiquity is full of such myths of divinities that die and rise again; we find them not only in Canaan but also in Babylon and Egypt. Israelite faith regarded this as an abomination. But now the prophet sees no difference in structure, between the complacent way his people take it for granted that they can be rid of their sins through God's mercy automatically, and the heathen belief in resurrection.

And he hears God answering (Hos. 6:4): 'O Ephraim, how shall I deal with you? How shall I deal with you Judah? Your loyalty to me is like the morning mist, like dew that vanishes early.' That is to say, God is telling them their repentance is a matter of a brief liturgical second, not a matter involving their everyday reality. What can God do? If justice and righteousness are to remain meaningful, what can he do but let the entire sinful people, for all their liturgical talk of repentance, be at the mercy of the destruction which it has itself brought about by its own sacrilegious behaviour? So the prophets shouted this unpopular proclamation of damnation, for all to hear.

The political catastrophes of the two Israelite states (the total destruction in 733 and 721 of the Northern Kingdom by the Assyrians, the crushing in 587 of the Southern Kingdom and the deportation of the upper classes to Babylon), left in Israelite tradition a very deep and remaining impression of the truth of the prophets' preaching and consequently of the truth of the old fundamental principle 'Righteousness exalts a nation, but sin is a reproach to any people' (Prov. 14:34). And yet historical experience, in the long run, did not tally with this principle. In Israel's history the results did not square, either in terms of good or evil, with the effects which might have been expected from Israel's actions.

Furthermore, where gradually this principle of the causal relationship between 'doing' and 'faring' came to be applied by individual Israelites to themselves, many of the calculations simply did not work out. Hitherto, then, in the course of the history both of the people as a whole and of individual members of the race, there could not yet have come into effect the direct complete balance which God had pledged to introduce. History, far from it, was virtually crying out for a fulfilment of all the happenings which had not been complemented and balanced out. Belief in God's power and will remained valid, and people believed that he would fully establish justice, reward the loyalty of his just believers by saving them from their foes and by giving them eternal life and salvation, and that he would punish the disloyalty of all sinners with eternal damnation. Since this belief remained, there developed in Israelite tradition the expectation of a future general Last Judgment Court held by God. Then God will, it was believed, completely fulfil all hitherto unfulfilled discrepancy between justice and salvation and between sin and damnation, and so he will judge every man according to his deeds; that is, he will assign all the actions of people to their corresponding eternal reward, evil will be consigned to eternal damnation, good will lead to eternal salvation.

In carrying out his judgment, God will bring into full effect his own justice and righteousness, as he has promised in choosing his Chosen People; so that the carrying out of judgment is at the same time a *glorification* of God the Lord.

Regarding the Last Judgment, therefore, the old belief was still held, in the eschatology (doctrine of the expectation of the last things) of later Israelite faith, the belief that God's actions and human actions correspond, in as much as human actions find their fulfilment in God's actions, if not in the past or present, at least in the future.

### (d) *Resurrection and Judgment*

This outlook, in its later eschatological extension, is the background for the expectation of resurrection, which, as has been said, only took shape at a late period in Israelite tradition. In order to make this clear, the following two texts should be compared, side by side:

'Blessed is the man who walks not in the counsel of the wicked, nor stands in the way of sinners, nor sits in the seat of scoffers; but his delight is in the law of the Lord, and on his law he meditates day and night. He is like a tree planted by streams of water, that yields its fruit in its season, and its leaf does not wither. In all that he does, he prospers. The wicked are not so, but are like chaff which the wind drives away. Therefore the wicked will not stand in the judgment, nor sinners in the congregation of the righteous; for the Lord knows the way of the righteous, but the way of the wicked will perish.' (Psalm 1:1–6, rsv)

'At that time shall arise Michael, the great (angel) prince who has charge of your people. And there shall be a time of trouble, such as never has been since there was a nation, till that time; but at that time your people shall be delivered, everyone whose name shall be found written in the book (of life). And many of those who sleep in the dust of the earth shall awake, some to everlasting life, and some to shame and everlasting contempt.' (Daniel 12, rsv)

The statements in the Psalm correspond fully to the old scheme; the doings of the just man find completion in a life in salvation; the sinner's evildoing finds its completion in ruin

and death. The resurrection prediction in the Book of Daniel,
the earliest unambiguous testimony to Israelite hope in
resurrection, does not say anything different. The Book of
Daniel was composed in the confusion of the Maccabean revolt
in the second century BC. The Syrian King Antiochus IV had
conquered Jerusalem on one of his campaigns, had desecrated
the temple by entering it, and had forbidden Jewish worship
(Dan. 11:21ff—168 BC). Following this catastrophic event the
different groups of pious people gathered together, under the
leadership of the Maccabeans, to wage partisan warfare, which
after some years led to success. Another group evidently
rejected military resistance, because it was expecting God's
intervention in the immediate future (cf. Dan. 11:32–35). The
apocalyptic Book of Daniel originates from this circle. In Israel
there were many people who in the preceding centuries had so
fallen prey to the influence of Greek culture that in the circles
of the pious they were regarded as defectors (Dan. 11:32). To
these people the present catastrophe seemed thoroughly
deserved: they saw it, indeed, as the beginning of the end of
time; they foresaw there will be much worse confusion, the
King of the North will advance against Jerusalem and
the Temple with his combined military forces (Dan. 11:36ff).
Then the guardian angel of Israel, Michael, will intervene from
heaven and save God's chosen people (Dan. 12:1). Yet that
will not be all the Israelites, but only the few who have loyally
preserved their righteousness intact throughout all the confusion. In God's heavenly book they are listed as those alone
who will live at the End (of time), whereas all sacrilegious
blasphemers will be overtaken by ruin and death. But not only
the Israelites then living, but all Israelites, including those who
are dead, will appear before God's Judgment Seat.

To appear at the Judgment, so says Daniel 12:2, they will be
awakened from death and, each according to his behaviour, be
assigned to everlasting life or to eternal shame. So resurrection
is here expected as the precondition for the carrying out of
God's Last Judgment on those who are already dead. If, for

men of old time, death formed the unquestioned limits before which God's reckoning was completed, adjusting the balance between a person's acts and his deserts, the more recent 'Apocalyptics' sought the complete fulfilment of this effective day of reckoning at some point beyond the frontier of death. For God's power over life could not be hindered by death, from fulfilling his promise to his righteous Chosen People; and, correspondingly, from implementing his 'anger' against all who have not been just and righteous. And so Daniel 12:2 is nothing but Psalm 1 in an 'eschatologicalized' form.

## 2. RESURRECTION OF THE DEAD IN JUDAISM

The concept of a resurrection as a miraculous restoration of dead persons to life may possibly have streamed from non-Jewish religion into the Jewish religion, and indeed the Iranian religion in particular has a distinctive doctrine of resurrection, whose age however, cannot be exactly determined, yet even if the idea may be in origin non-Jewish, at any rate the whole *context* and nexus of ideas, in which resurrection is discussed from the apocalyptic Book of Daniel onwards in Judaism, and the *function* which resurrection of the dead at the end of time serves within this framework, are both specifically Israelite in character.

It is not the resurrection as such which is here of importance, but what matters is that through the medium of resurrection God's Final Judgment can be implemented against the just and the unjust, so that no person's deeds may remain without their corresponding consequences in that person's fate. This is particularly valid for the Israelites as members of God's Chosen People: for each one of them, who in his earthly life has preserved justice and righteousness, God will carry out his initial promise of protection and salvation, promised to his people.

Interest is thus not focussed on the question as to what becomes of the dead, but on the question as to what becomes of those whom God chooses, what becomes of the might and honour of God, which he has pledged, put in pawn in choosing his Elect. So one can say that the question of *resurrection* in Jewish thinking stands in the *context* of the *theodicy* question. It is only to be thought of in a final deepest sense, as a question enquiring about the verification of the God of Israel's promise of what he will do for his people. 'Who God is' is decided for Israelite faith, by the evidence whether he has the power and the will to turn his word, which he has given, into comprehensive perfect reality. This explains why, in Jewish texts, we not only find very different conceptions of the resurrection of the dead at the end of time, but also come on testimonies speaking of the end of time without mentioning a resurrection.

The structure and the intention of the expectation of the end of time as such is always the same, however. Everywhere it is concerned with God's cause with his elect being finally brought to a satisfactory conclusion. It is concerned that those who through long trials have given proof of their fidelity, will attain a life which is eternal and everlasting, no longer threatened by any foes, a life with tangible redemption; and that on the other hand those who are unjust will be consigned to an eternal everlasting, irrevocable, death in damnation.

(a)  *Expectation of the Last Days without the Concept of Resurrection*

We will briefly present a few texts which know of no resurrection. One such text is the great hymn in praise of God's power to bring peace and salvation to his afflicted people, a later insertion in Isaiah 26. 'O Lord, thou wilt ordain peace for us, thou hast wrought for us all our works. O Lord our God, other lords besides thee have ruled over us, but thy name alone we acknowledge. They are dead, they will not live; they are shades, they will not arise; to that end thou hast visited them with destruction and wiped out all remembrance of them . . . O Lord, in distress they sought thee, they poured out a prayer when thy chastening was upon them. Like a woman with child, who writhes and cries out in her pangs, when she is near her time, so were we because of thee, O Lord; we were with child, we writhed, we have as it were brought forth wind. We have wrought no deliverance in the earth, and the inhabitants of the world have not fallen' (i.e. were not born) (Isaiah 26:12–14, 16–18, RSV).

Those praying here trust their God so completely that on the one hand in their prayer they see the foes who are oppressing them as already dead, and finished for all eternity; yet on the other hand they see themselves as people who are incapable of doing anything. And now their hope in God increases in the following statement: 'Thy dead shall live, their bodies shall rise. O dwellers in the dust, awake and sing for joy! For thy dew is a dew of light, and on the land of the shades thou wilt let it fall' (Isaiah 26:19, RSV).

Here God's help in need amid the distress of war is praised in the imagery of a miraculous powerful act of resurrection of the dead, an act through which the earth is forced to give up the shades of the dead which the earth has in her keeping. The thought is quite similar to that in the promise of the prophet Ezekiel (ch. 37) promising God's act of salvation for his chosen people, using the image of the resurrection of the skeletons in the valley or plain of dry bones.

Correspondingly the apocalyptic writer Enoch encourages the righteous to hope that their children will rise up and soar up like eagles (cf. Is. 40:31), whereas the sinners who are at present oppressing them will themselves be tormented (Enoch Apocalypse 96). And in the 'Assumption of Moses' in a hymn about God's Last Judgment (10:1ff) we read that God will arise to punish the heathen but Israel is promised that God will elevate Israel and let it hover among the stars in the firmament. If what we have here is the idea that Israel at the end of time will be elevated to *heaven* in order to be present as the community of the eternally saved and look from on high and see the destruction of their wicked foes on earth; what we have in the Book of Jubilees (23:29ff) is Israel being present at the spectacle, experiencing it on *earth*. Here the blessed end of time appears as the restoration of the patriarchial period of the beginning, so it is no problem for them to imagine that the bones of the just and righteous dead rest peacefully in the earth and that their spirits rejoice at the prospect of God passing judgment on his foes and dispensing his mercy and grace to his righteous people (v. 31). That all should arise at the resurrection is thus by no means an indispensable element of the future completion of salvation. Also the sects of the Essenes from Qmran, whose library of scrolls was found in 1947 in the mountains west of the Dead Sea, evidently are not acquainted with a resurrection at the end of time.

Only the grace of God, through which they who were sinners, nevertheless were reckoned among the selected community granted salvation at the end of time, is praised as an act of awakening from the dead (e.g. 1 QH 11:12).

### (b) *Resurrection for Judgment*

So, even in the texts which *do* speak about a resurrection at the end of time, it is important to pay close heed to the context in which the statement has its sense and its function. The closest to the passage from Daniel discussed above is a piece from the Enoch Apocalypse (ch. 22). On a visionary journey on foot through remote uninhabited stretches of the earth, in which the fallen angels are held captive, Enoch reaches the place of sojourn of the dead. There Enoch sees four 'hollow places' or cavernous rooms, three of them dark and one of them light (v. 1f). The angel who is guiding him explains to him that these 'hollow places' are different places of sojourn for the dead (v. 3f). After an interlude (vv. 5–7) the angel explains why the rooms are separated from each other. Firstly the room which is full of light is separated from the three dark ones, because here the spirits of the righteous are sojourning (v. 9). Of the three dark rooms the first one is set aside for sinners who have died and been buried and on whom no judgment has been executed within life. They are waiting here for their condemnation at the future Day of Judgment (v. 10f). The second dark room is meant for those who were killed 'in the days of the sinners' and are now lamenting to God because of this. These are the righteous who have been murdered and whose spokesman Abel has been previously introduced, in the interlude at verses 5–7. They are also awaiting the Last Judgment and the punishment of their murderers and the reward for their own justice and righteousness. The last 'hollow place' is reserved for the sinners who have joined forces with sacrilegious lawless transgressors (v. 12). Of this last group it is said that their spirits will not be punished at the Last Judgment nor raised from that place (v. 13). The sense of this apparently remarkable piece of information is made clear when attention is paid to the principle for dividing up the four groups of the dead. In the case of the second and third groups we are concerned with those whose earthly fate is in contrast to their deeds, and they are therefore going to have their cases cleared up at the future Last Judgment. There are, on the one hand, sinners whose wrongdoing has not been matched in their lifetime by their deserved ruin. On the other hand we have the righteous and just people whose violent deaths stand in glaring contrast to the justice of their righteous acts.

In contrast with this, in the case of the just group of the dead, there is no talk of any balance requiring to be restored at a final Day of Judgment. The light room in which they are sojourning, is to be thought of as their final resting place. They have thus obviously led lives which corresponded to their righteousness, so that, as the old stories of the patriarchs express it, their lives were simply made perfect in death, death rounded off their lives. Now if you notice that in both of the middle groups we have, standing facing each other, the sinners and the righteous who will appear at the Last Judgment, then it is not difficult to see that the first and the last mentioned groups belong together. For, as for the just, so too for the completely unjust, the Final Judgment is not relevant, as is expressly stated. That only makes sense, if one assumes the reference is to unjust sinners, who reaped their merited appropriate deserts already in their lifetime. They remain at the end in the darkness in which they now are, in the same way as the righteous spend their eternal sojourn in the place full of light, where Enoch sees them. So it can be seen that this section which at first glance appears like many apocalyptic texts to be confused and obscure, is in fact well thought out and balanced in its structure, and this structure reflects the principle, which we described above, underlying the old view of the correspondence between what one does and what one has to endure, between one's actions and one's condition.

It is interesting that the old idea, (according to which there is 'correspondence' or 'equivalence', whereby the 'acts' and their corresponding 'deserts', are balanced out in a person's lifetime), is found alongside the more recent idea according to which, the corresponding sides will only be balanced up at the Last Judgment. One sees clearly that the one is seen as a supplement to the other. The Final Judgment will only affect those whose acts did not receive their due deserts in their lifetime. God as Final Judge will not do anything different from what the older conception held he would do in earthly life, namely, that God is there to make sure that the sacrilegious go to damnation and the righteous obtain the salvation which by their doings they have merited. The expectation of the end, therefore, does not, as is often assumed, contradict the old belief, which concentrates on this life; its goal is not the expectation that the end of time will usher in a total severance with all that has hitherto existed. The Final Judgment is rather awaited in the expectation that it is the final squaring of all unsettled accounts, settled beyond the limits of death and therefore a rounding-off of the history of mankind.

The Final Judgment will only mark a break in the course of history in so far as sacrilegious blaspheming evildoers experience happiness and success on earth, and righteous, just people endure oppression and suffering. The Final Judgment will mark a break with all the disproportion between a person's acts and his deserts hitherto noted in history. It will be a break which will redress the balance, restore the proper proportions, set things to right. So now the statement about resurrection which pops up so unexpectedly in the final sentence can be understood when it says that those who are completely and entirely evil will not be among those resurrected; that is to be understood in the sense of the idea in Daniel 12, according to which both the unjust and the just will be awakened to appear at God's Judgment. This is quite as unnecessary for those who are thoroughly evil, as it is for those who are just, mentioned in the first group. Since in both cases the balance between acts and deserts has already been established in their lifetime, they do not need to attend the Last Judgment and so do not need to be raised from the dead. Here we have to add, as far as the two middle groups are concerned, that in so far as *they* have to attend the future Judgment, *they* also will have to be raised from the dead. So the resurrection of the dead stands in closest relationship with the Final Judgment. The raising of the dead has, so to speak, a 'feeder' function, furnishing those who are to be judged.

And since this context in Enoch 22 is so unreflectingly taken for granted in the sense we have in Daniel 12, it can be assumed that this was a widely held basic assumption in the apocalyptic circles of that time. For the sake of completeness it must also be pointed out that the same pattern of a corresponding link between earthly and eschatological balance, between acts and deserts, is found elsewhere too without reference to resurrection. In the section Enoch 102 to 104 (see Charles, II, 273–277) there is the same division into four groups as in Enoch 22 but the suffering just and righteous people are there promised salvation and their oppressors who have hitherto been successful are promised damnation, without any explanation that first of all they would be raised from the dead in order to face this judgment.

The predominant interest is focussed on the certainty that God will carry out his promise of salvation to his chosen people, and so will also deliver all rebellious, disloyal, unfaithful backsliders and blaspheming sacrilegious evildoers to their justly merited damnation. God intends that just and righteous behaviour will lead to life, and that unjust behaviour brings death in its wake (Ps. 1); and God will ensure that he is not thwarted in his vigilance by the course of history, by showing himself in due time to be the Lord over history. This is the focus of Jewish expectation of the end of the world.

(c) *Resurrection of the Just to Eternal Life*

It is in keeping with this focus of interest, that in most of the texts, in which the concept of a resurrection of the dead at the end of time appears, there is not a mention of sinners arising for the Last Judgment, but only mention of the righteous, who are awakened from the dead to receive that life of salvation to which they are entitled. So for example in the Testament of Judah (ch. 25) there is vividly depicted the resurrection at the end of time of the progenitor of the tribe Jacob-Israel and his twelve sons. These twelve sons are placed as princes over the twelve tribes, which can now henceforth live without sin or error in peace and happiness. 'Those who have died in grief shall arise in joy, and those who were poor for the Lord's sake shall be made rich, and they who have been in want shall be filled, and they who have been weak shall be strong, and those who are put to death for the Lord's sake shall awake to life' (cf. Testament Benjamin 10; Testament Zebulun 10).

According to Enoch 91:10f and 92:3–5 the righteous will arise from the sleep of death and receive from God the limitless possibility of living in righteousness, whereas all sinners are to be banned into utmost darkness. Enoch 51 describes how that is to be thought of: 'And in those days shall the earth also give back that which had been entrusted to it, and Sheol also shall give back that which it has received, and hell shall give back that which it owes. For in those days the Elect One shall arise, And he shall choose the righteous and holy from among them for the day has drawn nigh that they should be saved' (Enoch 51:1–2; see Charles, II, 218). Incidentally, the Messiah is also

named, and he, God's Elect One, will rule as God's governor
among the righteous who have been raised from the dead, yet
he is not expressly spoken of as one of these righteous who have
been raised from the dead. The connection with the expectation
of the Day of Judgment emerges especially clearly in the
description in the Ezra Apocalypse: After terrible catastrophes
which usher in the end of time, from heaven there appears the
glorious perfect heavenly City of Jerusalem and comes down to
earth, and for four hundred years the Messiah will rule over
the righteous survivors of the confusion and disturbances.
Then the Messiah and his companions shall all die. 'Then shall
the world be turned into the primaeval silent seven days, like as
at the first beginnings' (Ezra 7:30; see Charles, II, 582). Then
eternity begins. It commences with a general resurrection of
the dead followed by the Final Judgment at which only those
who have been pious observers of the faith and done deeds of
righteousness will be saved. Sinners on the other hand shall
inevitably perish (Ezra 7:26–44; see Charles, II, 582–584).

A similar vision is described in the Apocalypse of Baruch
(2 Baruch 30:1–5; see Charles, II, 498). In Baruch, however,
the Messiah does not die, but returns to heaven. 'Then all who
have fallen asleep in hope of Him shall rise again. And it shall
come to pass at that time that the treasuries will be opened in
which is preserved the number of the souls of the righteous,
and they shall come forth, and a multitude of souls shall be
seen together in one assemblage of one thought, and the first
shall rejoice and the last shall not be grieved. For they know
that the time has come of which it is said, that it is the
consummation of the times. But the souls of the wicked, when
they behold all these things, shall then waste away the more.
For they shall know that their torment has come and their
perdition has arrived' (2 Baruch 30:2–5; see Charles, II, 498).

(d) *Corporeal Resurrection*

What is being discussed here is the awakening of the souls of
the righteous. They are awakened from sleep in order to arise

and leave their graves, whereas the wicked have to remain in their graves (cf. Book of Jubilees 23, mentioned above at p. 87). Is the idea then that there is no thought of *bodily* resurrection? Is the conception one of destinies being worked out only in a purely spiritual sphere? As is the case with the idea of the expectation of resurrection in general, so too this aspect has not been elaborated in any precise detail.

Yet it would be a misunderstanding of the text to regard it as making a distinction between a purely spiritual mode of existence for those who have arisen from the dead and the bodily state of existence in their preceding life. The stress is not laid on any idea that they are souls which arise without their bodies, in the way Socrates in his platonic manner praised the advantage of bodily death as bringing release of the human soul from the inappropriate fettering shackles of the body. Widespread though such a contempt for the body may have been—particularly in New Testament times in the contemporary Hellenistic world—such an attitude was impossible for a Jew. The Jewish experience of life was too earthly and concrete, and the attitude to God was similarly too down-to-earth and too concrete, for the Jewish concept of God's final perfect salvation, reserved for God's chosen ones, to have been envisaged in such an abstract way, or framed as an abstract expectation.

Accordingly, we can only regard this mention of the resurrection of 'souls' or 'spirits' as nothing more than a completely naive unreflecting use of a general imprecise popular anthropological concept. According to this idea a human being is a body with a soul and alive, not a soul surrounded by a body. The modern medical man can only be absolutely delighted with Old Testament anthropology. Psychological concepts all have a somatic reference and a somatic function, just as similarly the other way round it is inconceivable for the Israelites that anything is purely physical in quality, for the human being as a whole, with his body and soul, is 'flesh'. Just as the soul is the life imbuing the body with life, so too the body is the soul's arsenal for action: body and soul are most intimately linked.

Correspondingly, only a person who is alive in the body is really in the full sense a human being, and God is a God of the living, not of the dead. The dead are regarded as entities formerly alive now deprived of strength and fading away, divorced from the reality of life and isolated by themselves. Extremely significantly and impressively too we read in the Book of Job for example: 'If a man die, shall he live again? . . . Thou prevailest for ever against him, and he passes; thou changest his countenance, and sendest him away. His sons come to honour, and he does not know it; they are brought low, and he perceives it not. He feels only the pain of his own body, and he mourns only for himself' (Job 14:14 and 20–22, RSV).

Anyone who has this conception of a human being does not hold that an expectation of the promise of salvation made by his God is to be fulfilled in some abstract lifeless existence. Although in most of the resurrection texts in Judaism there is missing any reference to the manner in which the resurrection occurs, and there is missing too any clear anthropological conception, nevertheless we have an adequately realistic expression of views about the future salvation awaiting those who shall arise from the dead at the end of time. The expectation held is one of salvation which admittedly far surpasses all expectations hitherto entertained, but nevertheless even the most 'transcendent' salvation is expected to be extremely concrete as far as it concerns the living individuals themselves. Although the physical aspect of resurrection is never raised as a topic on its own account, such a discussion does not even arise where it is expressly expounded on one occasion in the Apocalypse of Baruch (chs. 49–51; see Charles, II, 508–509). The seer takes as his starting point the fact that God shall awaken the righteous and the wicked to his Day of Judgment (cf. Dan. 12:11, Enoch 22 and similar texts). But he is concerned about the question whether at the resurrection sinners can return at all into the bodies with which they have

sinned. Sin has, after all, desecrated the body created by God!
Will God therefore not have to transform the bodies at the
resurrection of the dead at the end of time? God's answer
confirms this, but it distinguishes between resurrection and
judgment. In a first act, all the dead will be raised in the form
in which they lived and acted: human beings will see each
other all present as they were. For God's judgment shall be
passed on them all in accordance with what they have done in
their earthly life. And according to whether God recognizes
them as righteous or sinners, he will transform them, in a
second act, so that their form or 'aspect' now corresponds to the
final definitive sentence which their judge has passed on them.
The righteous shall then appear in glorious shining beauty and
the wicked will look ugly and repulsive.

Aesthetics are here pressed into the service of theological
reflection, for the main concern here is that the deliverance of
the righteous into the perfect salvation of God, is effective
to the point of transforming their appearances; and, correspondingly, the departure of the wicked into eternal damnation
is reflected in their transformation too. The drastic separation
of the righteous and the wicked at God's Last Judgment is
matched by a corresponding intensification within the bodily
constitution of human beings: goodness has the effect of
producing radiant beauty; wickedness on the other hand
produces nauseating ugliness. So these reflections of a Jewish
theologian of a relatively later period (towards the end of the
first century AD), show how salvation and damnation, allotted
after the resurrection by verdict of God's Last Judgment, were
taken for granted in a concrete physical sense, and how
seriously they were viewed.

(e)  *Resurrection of Christians in the New Testament*
. Let us attempt to compare the results of our survey hitherto
with the corresponding views expressed in the New Testament.
It has to be recognized that the primitive Christian expectation
of a resurrection of the dead at the end of time is thoroughly

Jewish in character. This is firstly and above all true of Paul. Precisely in the same way as for the Jewish writers we have discussed, for Paul it is a conception he takes for granted that in the future there will take place God's Final Judgment (cf. Romans 2:6ff), and in this connection the dead will be resurrected (2 Cor. 5:10). For Paul too, God is the Almighty who 'makes the dead live and summons things that are not yet in existence as if they already were'(Romans 4:17, NEB). This is a formulation which clearly echoes the first two benedictions in the Jewish daily prayer quoted earlier.

Admittedly Paul has difficulty in acquainting his formerly heathen Christian communities with this Jewish inherited tradition of expectation. For, to them, unlike Paul, hope in a future resurrection was by no means self-evident. From Thessalonica he had received an anxious enquiry, when the first deaths occurred in the Christian community there, asking whether the deceased brethren shall not participate in the reunion of the Christians with Christ which is to take place. Paul seeks to console them and to free them from this anxiety by expounding to them that at the beginning of the events at the end of time Christ shall descend from heaven as the Triumphant Lord to be reunited with his followers, and then the deceased Christian brethren shall arise and will go to meet their Lord at the head of the procession of the redeemed to celebrate his welcome (1 Thess. 4:13–18). So he gives them the same answer as can be read in the Apocalypse of Baruch: 'they shall come forth, and a multitude of souls shall be seen together in one assemblage, of one thought, and the first shall rejoice and the last shall not grieve . . .' (2 Baruch 30:2; see Charles, II, 498). In the same way as the Seer of the Apocalypse of Enoch (92:2; see Charles, II, 261), 'Let not your spirit be troubled on account of the times; for the Holy and Great One has appointed days for all things', gives consolation, so too Paul gives consolation to his Christian community regarding the resurrection to come.

But when Paul seeks to explain expectation of the resurrection of the deceased brethren in terms of belief in Christ's resurrection (1 Thess. 4:14) there are no similarly unambiguous parallels in the Jewish texts. Yet, nevertheless, it can be pointed out that the Jewish apocalyptic writer is also acquainted with a special hope of salvation for the righteous, a hope for resurrection to life, a hope directed to the Messiah. In the Apocalypse of Baruch (30:2) it is stated that 'all who have fallen asleep in hope of Him shall rise again' (see Charles, II, 498). So Paul in a completely Jewish way, in 1 Corinthians, can defend the corresponding negative thesis that if the dead are not raised, then 'those who have died within Christ's fellowship are utterly lost. If it is for this life only that Christ has given us hope, we of all men are most to be pitied' (1 Cor. 15:17–19, NEB).

When Paul, on the other hand, with remarkable assurance proclaims the opposite of the previous truth (cf. 1 Peter 1:21), that too is an essential motif which has its exact equivalent in Jewish tradition. Just as Paul expects that Christ will rule surrounded by his own followers, and God will subject all his foes to him (1 Cor. 15:25) so too the writers of the Apocalypse of Ezra and the Apocalypse of Baruch likewise expect this, admittedly only of those living at the time of the appearance of the Messiah (Ezra 7:27f; see Charles, II, 582: Apocalypse of Baruch 29:3–30; see Charles, II, 497–498). But, both in the Letter to the Thessalonians and the Letter to the Corinthians, Paul wants to stress that it is the special hope of the Christians that *their* dead would be resurrected at the coming of Christ already in order to share with the living in his rule as Lord at the end of time. Paul does not speak of a general resurrection of the dead. Paul's conception of the way in which the resurrection will have its effect on the bodies of people corresponds to the ideas in the Apocalypse of Baruch (49–51; see Charles, II, 508–509) outlined above (pp. 93-96).

The dead will be raised, and 'time shall no longer age them' (2 Baruch 51:9; see Charles, II, 509) or, as Paul says, 'the dead will rise immortal' and the living will be 'clothed with immortality', transformed in glorious splendour (1 Cor. 15:52,

NEB). Likewise, the writer of the Apocalypse then stresses that the righteous who are allotted eternal life are transformed in their bodily existence: 'their splendour shall be glorified in changes, and the form of their face shall be turned into the light of their beauty' (2 Baruch 51:3; see Charles, II, 508). For the writer is convinced that the present bodies 'which are now involved in evils, and in which evils are consummated' (2 Baruch 49:3; see Charles, II, 508) are not able to receive and preserve the splendour of eternal glory unless they are first transformed (v. 2). Similarly Paul states: 'flesh and blood can never possess the Kingdom of God, and the perishable cannot possess immortality' (1 Cor. 15:50, NEB). Nevertheless Paul unfolds 'a mystery', namely, that 'this perishable being must be clothed with the imperishable and what is mortal must be clothed with immortality' (1 Cor. 15:53). This is the same as the way in which, in the Apocalypse of Baruch, those who are now righteous, by their future transformation into glory shall be able to 'acquire and receive the world which does not die which is then promised to them' (2 Baruch 51:3; see Charles, II, 508).

And as Paul knows that the Christians through their bond with their risen Lord already share bodily in the glory of the end of time, he is all the more emphatic in his warnings to the Christians not to 'desecrate' their bodies through intercourse with harlots, that is, he is warning them not to eradicate the 'honour' conferred on them and their bodies of sharing in the resurrected body of Christ the Lord in his glory, not to extinguish this honour by sexually sharing the body of a prostitute (1 Cor. 6:12–20). When at Mark 12:26f the resurrection of the dead is accounted for by the fact that God, who chose Abraham, Isaac and Jacob, is a god of the living and not of the dead, then this in turn corresponds, as we have seen, to the primitive Israelite belief in God expressed in the Jewish Eighteen Benedictions prayer.

Luke even goes so far as to have Paul appear as basically the representative of the Pharisee hope of resurrection persecuted and accused by the High Council (Acts 23:6f; cf. 24:14f, 20f; 26:6f, 21–23). This shows the extent to which, as far as the post-Pauline generation is concerned, the real core of their own Christian belief could be represented by the Christians as being what was also in their view the core of Jewish traditional faith; with the result that the Jews are persecuting the representatives of their own central hope of resurrection when they persecute the Christians. This is right to the extent that primitive Christian hope of resurrection and the eschatological sphere encompassed by their expectation do reveal that it is a thoroughly Jewish heritage.

### 3. THE RESURRECTION OF THE MESSIAH JESUS IN THE FRAMEWORK OF JEWISH EXPECTATION OF RESURRECTION

#### (a) *Resurrection of the Messiah*

Although we have thus seen from the Jewish texts that the Christian hope of resurrection is domiciled in Judaism, and Christian statements cannot be understood without comprehension of this, nevertheless, the results of our examination are disappointing as regards the centre of primitive Christian belief, namely the *Resurrection of Christ*. For, nowhere do the Jewish texts speak of the resurrection of one individual which would have already taken place before the resurrection of the righteous at the end of time, and distinct from and separate from the latter. Nowhere in the texts either does the participation in salvation by the righteous at the end of time depend on their belonging to the Messiah who has previously been raised as the first to be resurrected by God, 'the first fruits of the harvest of the dead' (1 Cor. 15:20, NEB). But this is the very thing which is thoroughly characteristic of the primitive Christian hope of salvation.

Paul can, it is true, say in a thoroughly Jewish way, that there would not even be Christ's resurrection if the thesis put forward by opponents in Corinth were correct when they maintain that fundamentally there is no resurrection of the dead (1 Cor. 15:12ff). This throws into relief the fact that the Christian basic proclamation of the resurrection of the crucified Messiah (1 Cor. 15:3f) is thought within the framework of the Jewish hope of resurrection. The event of Christ's being raised from the dead appears to him as the anticipation of the beginning of the resurrection of the dead at the end of time. At the end of time, which is close, the resurrection of Christians will follow this (1 Cor. 15:23f). But such a special resurrection in advance of the end of time by the mediator of salvation does not appear to be known in Judaism. All we have found is the expectation that the righteous will be revived when the Messiah appears. According to Enoch (51:3–5; see Charles, II, 218–219) the throne of the Messiah is at the centre of the life of the righteous who have been resurrected, and it is the source of their joy. And when according to the vision of the Apocalypse of Ezra and that of Baruch only the living share the first period of lordship with the Messiah, the living still die, according to Baruch, thereafter 'all who have fallen asleep in hope of Him shall rise again' (2 Baruch 30:2; see Charles, II, 498), that is to say that at his second coming which follows and is final, namely at the Final Judgment, the Messiah will give the righteous the eternal life of salvation. This corresponds to the primitive Christian hope that the risen Christ will reveal himself as their Saviour before God's Judgment (1 Thess. 1:10), so that in their faith in Jesus they may have hope of their share in God's future salvation at the end of time (1 Peter 1:3ff). Indeed, according to the Apocalypse of Ezra, (Ezra 7:29; see Charles, II, 582), at the end of his 400 years' reign, the Messiah 'shall die, and all in whom there is human breath'. From this we are to conclude that the Messiah also belongs to those who are raised from the dead after the seven days of 'primaeval silence' (4 Ezra 30f; see Charles, II, 582). But unfortunately this is not explicitly stated.

The Day of Judgment described in the following section of Ezra (v. 33ff), is carried out by God himself: the Messiah has no further function (cf. likewise Rev. 20:11ff!). Probably what we have here is a secondary working together of two differing concepts: the concept of the Messiah's rule as Lord, and the concept of God's Final Judgment. The expectation of resurrection belongs to the latter concept, and has nothing to do with hope in the Messiah. In the Jewish tradition the concepts are sparse and not balanced, in the very area on which the interest of primitive Christianity is concentrated, namely, on the connection between the resurrection of the Messiah and the resurrection of his followers and their sharing in salvation. Certain ideas beginning to move in that direction can be found which may have furnished points of departure for the Christian ideas. Yet if this were the only bridge leading from the Jewish hope of resurrection to the Christian belief in the risen Messiah, then this bridge would be extremely narrow and fragile, hardly suitable to explain the origins of primitive Christianity's Easter faith, a faith which essentially is faith in Christ.

## (b) *The Translation of Enoch*

There are two other tracks to be followed in the Jewish tradition with regard to our question. The first leads us to the presumable origin of the idea of the appearance of the Messiah in the midst of the righteous resurrected at the end of time, as described in Enoch 51 (cf. above p. 92). At the end of the section (of what could be termed 'parables'), to which chapter 57 belongs, there is an appendix (chs. 70, 71) which probably represents a separate strand of tradition of its own. This can be seen from the use of the same material at another place in the Book of Enoch (14:8ff) for a different context.

At Enoch 70 and 71, following Genesis 5:24, we find an account of the Translation of Enoch right from out of the midst of his earthly life. He becomes the Messiah, who as at several places in the preceding parables is here referred to as the 'Son of Man', and is thereby elevated to God (Enoch 70:1f). That is the superscription over the following personal account by Enoch. First of all Enoch is raised aloft to 'the place for the elect and righteous' (v. 3). And sees 'the first fathers and the righteous who from the beginning dwell in that place' (v. 4). This surely is intended to evoke the idea of something like the 'hollow space' which is mentioned, at Enoch 22, as the eternal place of sojourn for the righteous (cf. p. 88f above). In a second translation he is then raised up into heaven (71:1). There he sees the angels, and 'two streams of fire', and he falls on his face before God (71:1–3; see Charles, II, 235–236). The archangel Michael shows him all 'secrets', that is, everything in God's Kingdom which is inaccessible to human earthly perception. He sees the guardians of God's throne and the myriads of angels who form God's royal household (71:3–8). God surrounded by his angels comes forth from his heavenly house. Enoch once again prostrates himself and with 'trans-figured' voice he blesses and glorifies and extols (71:9–12). Then God (according to Charles, II, 237, 'the angel') comes to Enoch and he greets him with His Voice, and says unto him: '*Thou art* the Son of Man, who *art* born unto righteousness, and righteousness abides over *thee*. And the righteousness of the Head of Days forsakes *thee* not' (Enoch 71:14).*

This address to Enoch is like the words spoken to Jesus at his baptism (Mark 1:11; cf. 9:7) but the scene in heaven corresponds to the description of Christ's appearance as the slaughtered lamb in Revelation (4f) and presumably this is just the way primitive Christianity envisaged Christ's Ascension (Phil. 2:9–11; Romans 1:4). The form of address used to Enoch, calling him 'the Son of Man', evidently places Enoch in the position and function of the heavenly Messiah, of whom frequent mention was made in the preceding parables. So when the heavenly scene is described (71:1ff) mention is no longer made of the Son of Man at God's side (70:1). In as much as Enoch was taken away to the Son of Man, he has entered into his role. So God proclaims eternal peace to him (71:15) and proclaims his function. 'And all shall walk in thy ways since

---

* *Translator's note:* Wilckens interprets the more difficult reading here, whereas Charles's emendation (II, 237: '*This is . . . is . . . him . . . him . . .*') is not now widely accepted.

righteousness never forsaketh *thee*: with *thee* will be their dwellingplaces, and with *thee* their heritage, And they shall not be separated from *thee* for ever and ever and ever. And so there shall be length of days with that Son of Man, And the righteous shall have peace and an upright way in the name of the Lord of Spirits for ever and ever' (Enoch 71:16–17; see Charles, II, 237).*

Enoch is here described as perfect in righteousness and all the righteous will assemble round him. In so far as they are still on earth he is their hope and the goal of their path; in looking up to him they already have in sight what their reward, as justified in righteousness, will be in eternity. He is their heavenly ideal, and their example demonstrating the coming into effect of eternal salvation at the end of time, showing the destiny the righteous can expect as the lot corresponding to their actions. He is the first one perfect in righteousness—just as the risen Christ, according to 1 Cor. 15, is the first of those to be raised from the dead at the end of time and as such is the heavenly guarantor of the Final Salvation awaiting Christians (1 Peter 1:3ff)! The function into which Enoch, translated, is inducted in heaven, corresponds to the function of the ascended Christ. That there is in truth a relationship here, is shown by many sayings of Jesus in the Gospel tradition in which Jesus represents himself as the Coming Son of Man (cf. especially Luke 12:8f; Matthew 19:28). At Mark 14:62, Jesus expressly confesses to the High Court he is the Son of Man (cf. Dan. 7:13) who has been installed as Lord in heaven (according to Ps. 110:1); and this is the way the martyr Stephen sees him at the moment before his death (Acts 7:55f).

Yet Enoch is translated from out of the midst of his earthly *life* and elevated to be the Son of Man, whereas Jesus is raised from his *death*. Yet there is no mention of a resurrection as a precondition of his installation on his throne in heaven in the function of the mediator of salvation at Enoch 70f: just as there

---

* *Translator's note:* Wilckens takes the more difficult reading *thy, thee*: Charles 'restores' *his* and *him*.

is no mention of how the Jewish documents referring to resurrection know the concept of a resurrection of the Messiah.

### (c)  *The Resurrection of the Prophet Elijah*

We progress a stage further however, if we follow a second track. According to Enoch 70:2, Enoch was 'raised aloft in the chariots of the Spirit' to heaven. The translation of Enoch at Genesis 5:24 is hereby brought in line with Elijah's translation at 2 Kings 2:11. Elsewhere too in Jewish and early Christian tradition Enoch and Elijah appear together as the two Biblical transfigurations, occasionally they are also joined by Moses (cf. Mark 9:4).

Moses and Elijah are the 'two witnesses' spoken of in Revelation 11, and something remarkable is reported about them. They appear together and the Biblical miracles of old are repeated at the end of time; so they are invincible (Rev. 11:5f). After completion of their testimony however 'the beast that comes up from the abyss will wage war upon them and will defeat and kill them' (Rev. 11:7, NEB). Their corpses will lie unburied in the open street of the city for all to see, and the potentates of earth will congratulate each other on being rid of the two prophets (vv. 8–10). 'But at the end of the three days and a half the breath of life from God came into them; and they stood up on their feet to the terror of all who saw it. Then a loud voice was heard speaking to them from heaven, which said: "Come up here!" And they went up to heaven in a cloud, in full view of their enemies.' (Rev. 11:11–12, NEB). This passage has always been a riddle to commentators: and a great number of interpretations have been put forward, for example the suggestion that the seer of the vision intends in the image of Elijah and Moses to suggest the parallel of the two martyred apostles, Peter and Paul. But the only passage in the whole section remotely permitting such an interpretation is the remark at verse 8 referring to the scene of their martyrdom in the great city 'where also their Lord was crucified'. In other words Jerusalem. In view of this the author of Revelation would seem to be referring to two specific Christians when he speaks of two witnesses.

But then it is strange that the writer lets them undergo the same fate, resurrection and ascension, as Jesus their Lord. In the whole tradition of primitive Christianity this is unique, and does not fit into the usual framework which regards the resurrection of Christians as an event happening in the future at the end of time. Perhaps the author of Revelation means it in this sense too, and if so the passage would have to be understood as a prophetic prediction of the forthcoming martyrdom of both 'witnesses'. Then, however, the contradiction between this and the remainder of Christian tradition would be so great that one is at a loss to explain how a Christian of the end of the first century can have created this passage of his own accord. All difficulties disappear however if one sees it as a passage from Jewish tradition which the Christian author has taken over and transferred to apply to Christian conditions. And, as a matter of fact, there is nothing else specifically Christian in the whole section.

Even the resurrection after three and a half days is almost certainly not formed as an analogy to Christian statements about Christ's resurrection 'on the third day' or 'after three days'. What we have is a formulation of Jewish origin about resurrection (cf. Dan. 12:7, 13) which expressly refuses to be fitted into the framework of traditional Christian formulations. In this case the reference is to Moses and Elijah, and they play an important role elsewhere too in apocalyptic eschatology. What is of especial interest is that their translation into heaven is preceded by a destiny of suffering which culminates in their death and their resurrection which follows it. How it came to this can only be surmised.

Since time immemorial there was in Jewish tradition the concept that God sent Israel prophets who were, however, turned away, or indeed persecuted and killed. This motif is to be found in primitive Christian tradition repeatedly (cf. e.g. Matthew 23:29ff), and the Passion of Jesus was regarded in the early days as the culminating point of this suffering which is the fate of all emissaries of God (cf. e.g. 1 Thess. 2:15; Acts 7:51ff). Not only Elijah but especially Moses too, are both now regarded as prophets sent by God (concerning Moses cf. especially Deut. 18:15). So an obvious thing to do was to transfer the motif of the suffering and death of the prophets to them (cf. 1 Kings 19:10ff; Acts 7:35). If, however, what was said about their translation was taken together with what was said about their death, then this was only actually possible if one inserted the eschatological idea of resurrection here—since anyway the context of events discussed at Rev. 11 occurs shortly before the beginning of the end of time. That Elijah before the end of time will return to earth in order to set everything right was an expectation held since Malachi 4:5.

The disciples' question to Jesus at Mark 9:11 refers to this: when they ask 'Why do our teachers say that Elijah must come first?' (i.e. before the beginning of the end). Christ's reply is very strange: 'Yes, Elijah does come first to set everything right. Yet how is it that the scriptures say of the Son of Man that he is to endure great sufferings and to be treated with contempt? However, I tell you, Elijah has already come and they have worked their will upon him, as the scriptures say of him.' (Mark 9:12–13). That was originally taken to refer to John the Baptist; Jesus was understood to be saying that in John the Baptist there took place the return of Elijah and the Jews had treated him just as they had previously dealt with all the prophets. Now this conversation about Elijah's return takes place just after Jesus's command, which we discussed earlier, forbidding the disciples to spread the news of the vision they had been granted of Jesus in the company of Moses and Elijah (Mark 9:2–8) giving them strict orders not to reveal it till the time when 'the Son of Man had risen from the dead' (Mark 9:9). The disciples do not understand what is meant (Mark 9:10) and make the enquiry about the coming of Elijah (v. 11). This context becomes transparent and comprehensible only if one can assume that Mark is quietly taking issue with a tradition about Elijah from the circle of followers of John the Baptist, a tradition which was similar to the passage in Rev. 11, but which applied what is said there to John, so that accordingly they spoke of the violent fate of John and of his resurrection. Mark naturally toned this down, without devaluing the Baptist, whom he saw after all as preparing the way for Jesus (Mark 1:1f).

Accordingly, the argumentation remains a torso: the Son of Man who endures great sufferings (Mark 9:12) and who rises from the dead (Mark 9:9; cf. Mark 8:31) is according to Jesus none other than *Jesus*. But the returning Elijah was *John the Baptist* whose sufferings were, it must be admitted, similar to those of the Son of Man. That is not all, however. There is a second passage in Mark's Gospel (Mark 6:14–16) which confirms this. It is reported there that King Herod had heard of the work of Jesus and of the rumour coursing among the people, who 'were saying "John the Baptist has been raised to life, and that is why these miraculous powers are at work in him." And others said, "It is Elijah". Others again "He is a prophet like one of the old prophets". But Herod, when he heard of it, said, "This is John, whom I beheaded, raised from the dead!".' This is followed by a flashback to the horrible story of the death of John the Baptist (Mark 6:17–29). The story concludes with the remark, which is a singular analogy to the end of the story of Jesus's sufferings, that after the death of John the Baptist, his disciples came and took his body away and laid it in a tomb (Mark 6:29). Are we to believe that all this was thought up in the Christian tradition merely as a contrast to Christ's resurrection? That is difficult to believe. It is much more probable that we have here the reflection of a tradition that John the Baptist is Elijah who came again, died, was buried and rose again—like Elijah in Rev. 11. Mark represents this tradition as rumour among the people and dramatically lets the startled opinion come from the lips of Herod, the murderer of John the Baptist.

In a later passage in Mark he goes out of his way to repeat

the rumour among the people (Mark 8:27ff). When Jesus asks his disciples: 'Who do men say I am?', they answer, 'Some say John the Baptist, others Elijah, others one of the prophets.' With the popular rumours there is then contrasted Peter's confession of his belief that Jesus is the Messiah (Mark 8:29). This however does not clear up the question for Mark. Jesus himself adds that as the Son of Man he has to undergo great sufferings, be put to death and to rise again (Mark 8:31). If we view this against the background of the tradition of John the Baptist, of which we are reminded by verse 28, then it becomes clear how, in the view of Mark, it is Jesus and not John the Baptist, whose sufferings have been crowned by the resurrection. If this is correct, there is revealed behind the tradition of primitive Christianity a separate tradition concerning John the Baptist which maintained that in John the Baptist there took place the eschatological return of the prophet Elijah, and this tradition also saw John's death as also one in the series of violent fates of all the prophets, and taking over a motif from the Jewish tradition about Elijah, it proclaimed that John arose from the dead. If this is so, then we would be able to recognize in this picture of the Baptist a concrete claim being laid to a conception which is preserved in its original Jewish form at Revelation 11. Furthermore the motifs from this Jewish conception are to be found in surprising numbers in later tradition and especially in the popular writings of the Early Church.

## (d) *Synopsis*

The task set for this chapter was to find out how study of the Jewish expectation of resurrection can help us to understand the Christian preaching of resurrection. We can sum up in two points.

1. The hope cherished by the communities of early Christians of the resurrection of their dead at the end of time, corresponds by and large to Jewish expectations. But whereas in Judaism resurrection of the righteous as a consequence of

their just and righteous actions is what is hoped for, in Christianity resurrection is awaited as the effect of Jesus's resurrection in bringing salvation to those who belong to Christ in faith.

2. The primitive Christian proclamation of the resurrection of Jesus has no corresponding widespread previous existence in Jewish tradition. It is true that the Christian statements about the installation of Jesus as mediator in heaven of salvation for the redeemed and as judge of all the wicked, are statements which can be shown to be shaped by the character of the various forms of Jewish expectation of the Messiah, but there is no mention in Jewish tradition of the resurrection of the Messiah standing ready and waiting in heaven. There is only a narrow bridge leading to this from Jewish tradition in the observation, in one isolated Jewish text referring to the resurrection, that the prophet Elijah will return to set things aright in preparation for the events at the end of time, and will suffer the same violent death as all the prophets before him, but he will be raised from death. We have to add however that Elijah is never expressly given the function of the eschatological mediator of salvation.

Accordingly while the true character of the conceptual context of the primitive Christian hope in the resurrection can be illuminated by reference to the testimony of Jewish texts clarifying its Jewish setting, nevertheless there remains unresolved one outstanding problem involving the history of the tradition concerning the very core of the faith of primitive Christianity. This problem is that the proclamation of the resurrection of Jesus cannot be traced as derived from a correspondingly broad widespread direct tradition in Jewish belief. Thus we have here to a considerable and marked degree newly formed material. We can, it is true, trace elements from different sources which show that primitive Christian Christology is firmly bedded in Jewish tradition. The newly formed material is thus not *entirely* new in what it says. Nevertheless our search for the conditions under which there arose the primitive Christian proclamation of Jesus's resurrection draws a blank on all decisive points. Our enquiry evidently cannot be adequately answered in terms of the history of the transmission of the tradition of the faith in the Jewish homeland of primitive Christianity. Our enquiry requires a different answer, with which the following chapter is concerned.

## Chapter Three

# Origin and Significance of the New Testament Proclamation of the Resurrection

How can the emergence, the coming into being of the primitive Christian proclamation of the resurrection of Jesus be explained in historical terms?

### (a) *The Easter Events*

First of all we must enquire about the Easter events which form the basis for the earliest traditional account of Easter. According to our investigations in Chapter Two there are only two texts we must consider.

1. the Easter story at Mark 16:1–8 in its oldest form; and
2. the formulaic series 1 Cor. 15:5ff, in which the appearances of the risen Christ are enumerated.

As far as the transmission of tradition about Christ's appearances is concerned, the majority of researchers seem to be agreed in their verdict that at all events Christ's first appearance to Peter (1 Cor. 15:5) is a real experience, which probably happened to Peter in Galilee (Mark 16:7; cf. John 21:1ff). It is to be assumed that after Jesus's death Peter and the rest of Jesus's followers returned home to Galilee. Some time later there he experienced a vision, of the kind described by Paul at Galatians 1:15 as a 'revelation', in which Jesus appeared to Peter as the risen Christ and gave him the challenging command to gather together his disciples to form the community of the chosen companions in God's salvation at the end of time (cf. Luke 22:32). In this sense Peter became the rock on which the church will be built (Matt. 16:18). And in the command 'Feed my sheep' (John 21:15, 16, 17) there can be recognized a late echo of Peter's original function as leader.

The tradition links the appearance to Peter and the appearance to the group of the Twelve (1 Cor. 15:5; cf. Mark 16:7) and we have seen earlier, that in the earliest times they were the circle of leaders in the original Christian congregation in Jerusalem. To that extent, therefore, tradition has a historical core. Whether one can assume however that the Twelve were called to their vocations and positions as leaders by an appearance experienced by the whole group, is called into question by some Biblical commentators. In fact too the idea of a vision occurring to a whole group is not without difficulty, for in Jewish tradition, visions are always experienced by individuals and not by groups. If the group of the Twelve was already founded by Jesus himself before Easter, as the old tradition at Matthew 19:28 says, then some commentators find it easier to accept, that the Twelve were the first to be called together by Peter after he was granted the vision, and they looked on the fresh reconstitution of their group as based on the appearance experienced by Peter.

The same is then equally true of the appearance to over five hundred brethren (1 Cor. 15:6) who, we suggested above, should be identified as forming the core of the first congregation of Jesus's followers. The idea that their number was immediately three thousand as recorded at Acts 2:41, is an idealization; the idea of a later period. Yet it is probably historically correct at least that the founding of the primitive Church was predominantly due to the initiative of Peter and the Twelve and that the first Christian community right away had a rather large number of members, for the majority of the followers won by Jesus to his cause would, one can assume, have banded together after the surprising experience of his resurrection and formed a community.

On the other hand the vision of James cannot be contested on any convincing grounds. The fact that the tradition shows remarkable parallels to that about Peter, in that for example it is followed by an appearance to a group (1 Cor. 15:7), can be

explained from the tendency of the tradition to validate the
authority of Jesus's brother in the circle of 'all the apostles' in a
similar fashion to the authority of the circle of leaders of the
initial period. If on this account we were to dispute the historicity of the vision of James, this would be tantamount to gross
excess over normal healthy historical criticism. After all nobody
disputes Paul's vision. There were indeed thus several visions.

All these visions were not mentioned in the early period in
order to establish how the witnesses involved had experienced
the fact of Jesus's resurrection and so became the first believers.
This was admittedly taken for granted, but the *tradition* about
the appearances was concerned with the authorization of the
witnesses by the authority of the risen Christ. The appearances
are thus not really *testimonies* to the resurrection, but rather
*credentials* proving the identity and authority of the men who
because of their heavenly authorization had permanent authority in the Church, and that is why the accounts were handed
down in tradition. It was not within the framework of proclamation of the faith but within the ecclesiastical legal framework
that they were handed on. If however despite this intention behind the transmission of these traditional accounts, one still en-
quires whether the appearances did not actually *de facto* form the
basis of the faith of the witnesses, this probably only is applicable
in the case of Peter. For Peter was after all the first to whom
Jesus's resurrection was revealed. And if the situation of the
disciples of Jesus during the time after his ignominious end is
even approximately correctly described by Luke (cf. Luke
24:21) then there was great depression and resignation in the
circle. The first vision shown to Peter then would mark
the breakthrough, the beginning of new, renewed faith in
Jesus. Yet even this much is not completely certain. The words
of Jesus to Peter, handed down at Luke 22:31f, state that
Peter's faith will not fail; and when he 'is converted' (AV) or
has 'turned again' (RSV), or 'come to himself' (NEB), he is to
strengthen his brethren. This might be an indication that Peter
did not completely give up the cause of Jesus and return in

resignation to his former fisherman's life at the Sea of Galilee, but instead was attempting in some way or other to retain his faith in Jesus. The appearance which he experienced would then not have rekindled extinguished faith anew, but instead would merely have confirmed the faith which he had persisted in retaining.

If researchers are to a large degree in positive agreement up to this point, there is a further wide area of agreement in a negative sense about the Easter story according to Mark. It has already been indicated that this account is regarded by many commentators as a legend with a tendentious bias which arose at a late date. Our investigation has shown that what we are dealing with is probably an old tradition about the Easter conclusion of the account of the Passion, a tradition which arose in the early original Jerusalem Christian community. In terms of its literary form even so it is more precise to describe it as a legend rather than a cult legend. Cult legends are narratives intended to be read out or recited in divine worship which spring up and are handed down in such a context. This story does very probably indicate a 'cultic' function. The occurrence of the raising from the dead of the crucified Christ is here proclaimed from the lips of the angel to the assembled community, as the conclusion of the preceding story of Christ's sufferings. It proclaims that Christ as God's representative, the Righteous One, has been freed by God's mighty act and raised on high out of all his suffering and all the affronts and humiliation to which his human foes have subjected him.

When we enquire about the historical core of this story, the interpretation just given means we do not have such an easy solution as the many critics who, on account of their view that it is of late origin and has tendentious apologetic bias, feel that they can simply say there is no historical basis at all. For if it is an old tradition, then its unhistoricity cannot be taken for granted. What we have to do is to test it according to all the rules of the art of interpretation. We must take as our starting-point the tomb. This locale is fixed, and at the same time it stresses the substratum of the story, and as such it is even mentioned by Paul. It is hardly conceivable that this story was elaborated in Jerusalem and remained constant in the tradition if the tomb in the rock, about which it relates, did not actually exist. Indeed it is striking that the harsh Jewish polemics against the Christian proclamation of the resurrection, which are revealed in Matthew's account of the tomb, do not contest the tomb, as such, but they argue that the disciples used wilful deceit and stole the body of their Master, and that this is the real reason why the tomb was empty. Thus the actual tomb did exist and was surely held in reverence by the Christians. More than this; if we are right in judging that the Passion account was read out in divine service then we are led to the supposition that the setting for the final scene of the Passion account could also have been the setting for the divine service.

Then the angel's command, 'Look, there is the place where they laid him' (Mark 16:6), would have a definite concrete 'cultic' connection. In Jewish tradition there are many examples of documentary evidence showing that places of worship mentioned in traditional narratives are customarily explained in terms of extraordinary events which befell the founders of the cult there: these are known as 'aetiological cult legends'. Accordingly our supposition about the Easter story in Mark can be well substantiated on grounds of literary form.

If then Jesus's tomb, the empty tomb, is at the very least extremely probably a *fact*, then we must go on to enquire under what conditions the story arose. That the narrative sequence related was completely an invention, is entirely improbable. Perhaps we could envisage a story relating about the *disciples*, but not a story telling about the *women*, as possibly being a fabrication. The women are mentioned in the entire remaining tradition, except at Luke 8:2ff, only in the context of the events at the tomb. Later tradition shows a clear tendency to have the disciples at least confirm the women's discovery afterwards (Luke 24:12, 24; John 20:2f), and later tradition also has the disciples present on Easter Day in Jerusalem (Luke and John as compared with Matthew and John 21). Accordingly, it must be accepted that the core of the narrative is indeed that the women found Jesus's tomb empty in the early morning of the first day of the week.

Whether the vision of the angel was actually experienced by them, is clearly not susceptible to historical proof. The possibility must be left open that the women's discovery was only later given an Easter explanation in the light of the disciples' belief in the resurrection. After Christ's appearances in Galilee, the disciples, when they came to Jerusalem, came after all as the community of Christians believing in salvation through Jesus. It would not be surprising if they regarded the women's news of Jesus's empty tomb as a further sign of his resurrection, and in this belief they composed the story of the proclamation of Christ's resurrection by the angel at the empty tomb. Nowhere, till the latest tradition, is it stated that the discovery by the women was a cause effecting belief in the resurrection. Only John depicts the disciple 'whom Jesus loved', the disciple whom John introduces as the symbolic representative of true perfect belief and discipleship, as seeing the empty tomb, and, because of it, in contrast with Peter, believing (John 20:8). This demonstrates something that applies to the entire tradition, namely that this story serves to express faith in Jesus's resurrection, and not belief in his return to life. The way Jesus's tomb became empty is a question to which history cannot supply the answer. One can however at least refute some supposed explanations which have been repeatedly put forward since the Jewish polemics in antiquity. There is for example the 'rumour among the Jews' which Matthew combats, namely the story which 'became widely known, and is current in Jewish circles to this day' (Matt. 28:15) that the disciples had stolen the body of their Master. Hermann Samuel Reimarus, the first radical critic of the Gospels, in all seriousness declared this rumour to be accurate, but failed to find support, especially among other critical commentators. This applied also to the adventurous supposition, which survives even today in popular tradition, that Jesus was only in a state of suspended animation, only seemingly dead, lying in a trance, and that he later recovered and secretly left the tomb. This seems to have been used even in New Testament times as an argument against the Christian tradition. When at Mark 15:44f it is related that Pilate only let Joseph have the body after his officer had checked and confirmed that Jesus was dead, this highly unlikely detail is perhaps to be explained as a Christian answer to the suspicion of their opponents that Jesus was merely seemingly dead.

A third attempt by Jewish polemics to explain everything away is probably to be found reflected in what seems to be its New Testament echo in John's Gospel. When Mary in her sorrow thinks that the gardener may have in the meantime removed Jesus's body and laid it to rest elsewhere (John 20:15), this is in agreement with the Jewish argument of which we have evidence from a later period, that 'Juda the Gardener' actually did do this. In more recent times this explanation has been taken up, and refined in a most subtle, ingenious, not to say devious, manner. This argument runs as follows. Jesus was first of all as usual interred in a criminals' common grave. This is the spot which the women had made a note of and which they found empty on the morning of the third day. They had not realized, of course, that Joseph of Arimathea had meanwhile taken the body of Jesus and laid it to rest in his own tomb in the rock. The 'cloven-hoof' snag about this reconstruction of the events is that it is now necessary to go a step further and explain how the story at Mark 15:42ff arose.

It is argued that Joseph first of all kept quiet about his deed, out of pious consideration for the faith in the resurrection which had formed because of the discovery that Jesus's original burial place was empty, thus, this argument continues, Joseph's action only became known later, but could no longer imperil the firmly established belief in the resurrection, and so the tomb of Joseph easily became the traditional setting for the Easter story. The mesh of improbabilities, which have to be accepted if we believe such an explanation, is such an unlikely web of events that it without a doubt condemns itself. Although no historical argument can *prove* that Jesus's resurrection was the cause of the discovery of the empty tomb, similarly but conversely, no other kind of explanation of the empty tomb can *contest* the resurrection.

The historian in this respect is faced by proceedings upon which we can no longer shed light, and which, according to the conception underlying the primitive Christian tradition, were a series of events inaccessible to any such attempt to shed light on them. For, the resurrection itself, after all, was proclaimed as an event occurring at the end of time, and as such it was believed, by definition as it were, to be quite beyond comprehension at present. So for those of the early Christian period the empty tomb represented the place where it was appropriate to sing the praises of the risen Christ, but it was not regarded as proof of his resurrection. The appearances of Christ are in a similar position. Early Christian tradition regards them basically as revelations only applying to the person experiencing them (Gal. 1:15), and not accessible to anyone else. Whether they really happened, nobody even in those days could have afterwards checked. Admittedly no one then ever thought of making such a demand, for people in those days essentially accepted the possibility of such an extraordinary disclosure of 'hidden' reality made to select individuals as being part of the sphere of experience transmitted by tradition.

In the Jewish world, in which the earliest Christians lived, there was no greater, more certain authority than that of such a 'revelation'. Since the Greek view maintained that the world existed within itself, whereas the Jewish view believed that the world was a continuous lasting process of happenings, in which all 'doing' constantly provokes corresponding 'happening'; since furthermore God is not believed to be a being existing in self-sufficiency in a different remote world, but is believed to be Lord of this world in whose creative 'doing' the reality of this world consists, then it follows that the Jewish experience of the world was deeply determined by the possibility of ever new happenings and unexpected occurrences, and this attitude led to a receptivity for new actions by God and a new word from God. This indeed was an essential characteristic of Israelite faith. The demand for an investigation whether the person having the vision really experienced a vision, would doubtless have been rejected by the Christians of those days, as a completely incomprehensible senseless pointless desire.

Verification of the truth of a word received and proclaimed was, to Israel's way of thinking, always to be ascertained by the happenings that followed. Anyone hearing a message is looking forward into the future; for, when God speaks, it is done, when he commands it stands fast, according to Psalm 33:9. It corresponds to this outlook that the appearances of the risen Christ were experienced as calls to vocation and transmitted as such. The experience of the resurrection of Jesus, which was contained in the appearances, did not in itself simply refer back to the event of the resurrection, but evidently referred forward to the 'doing' corresponding to it. Similarly too as we have seen the idea of the resurrection of Jesus was bound up with the idea of Christ's installation at the end of time in his position of full power and authority beside God in 'concealment'. The reality of this 'concealment' in God's presence in heaven was as far as human beings were concerned still in the future.

The translation of Jesus, accordingly, is to be understood in the sense it has in the faith of primitive Christianity, namely as the 'superseding' of all future time, as the advance occurrence of events scheduled for the end of time. One would be able to see the risen Christ as was intended at the *end of time*, when God will, at a single stroke, reveal what is still concealed and bring his chosen people together with the Messiah. At the appointed time they shall see him as the mediator of their salvation and will rejoice (1 Peter 1:8f), but his foes will recognize him as their Judge who will consign them to damnation (cf. Mark 14:62). The 'seeing' as such is thus a matter for the end of time. The present is the time for believing, acting and hoping in his name, and in his *future* 'revelation' (1 Peter 1:8; Romans 8:24f; 2 Cor. 4:16–18). To the chosen few who *have seen* him (1 Cor. 9:1) he has appeared in order to call them to their vocation, and thereby set in motion the new mission on earth which corresponds to his rising from the dead. That is the view of the earliest Christians. Therefore, convinced as they were of Jesus's resurrection having taken place, nevertheless they equally felt themselves directed forwards and involved in a movement onwards.

(b)  *Theological Differences in the Exegesis of the Easter Testimony*

Our understanding remains extremely superficial, and we are failing to comprehend what was for contemporaries the essential point, if we concentrate our critical investigation solely on the question whether Jesus in a way that is demonstrably real actually did rise from the dead or not. The whole point of what the early tradition was getting at, when it asserted its occurrence, can only be estimated if one concentrates on understanding the *movement* into which the experience of the occurrence of Jesus's resurrection pushed the Church in primitive Christianity. The *consequences* following upon it, are what show the *truth* of Jesus's resurrection. It is only at the end of time and in the fullness of time at God's Day of Judgment that human discernment will comprehend the event of the resurrection. Then and only then shall we 'see him as he is' (1 John 3:2; cf. 1 Cor. 13:12).

The question as to the 'historicity' of the resurrection has been argued repeatedly, hither and thither for two hundred years, and I would certainly not wish to sweep it under the carpet, yet it seems to me irresponsible of some theologians to regard the New Testament mention of Jesus's resurrection simply as one means of expression of the experience of faith, for which there might equally well be substituted other interpretational devices ('*Interpretamente*', or 'interpretamenta', as W. Marxsen calls them). If a closer look is taken at what this thesis actually means, then it is revealed to be the constantly new awareness of

Jesus's presence experienced by Christians, it is the ever new and ever different form of the *reality* of encounter with Christ. Now of course this is an essential motif in the history of modern Protestant piety. Accordingly one should be cautious about blindly accepting it as the 'real' basic motif in the testimony to the resurrection made by the earliest Christians without seeing if this is the case. The primitive Christian references to Jesus's appearances, apart from the story of the appearance at Emmaus, are not at all concerned with risen Christ's contemporary *presence*. 'Jesus cometh this very day'—would not be the sort of heading which would give an accurate summary of the primitive Christian proclamation of the resurrection. The appearances were not handed down in tradition as disclosures of ever new encounters with the risen Christ, but as unique acts conferring legitimation of their authority to the first basic witnesses. After them there is no promise of an *encounter* with the risen Christ till the end of time.

Where motifs appeared in Paul's Christian communities, which moved the future coming of Christ at the end of time back into the present experience of the faith, Paul resisted strongly. But where the reality of Christ's resurrection is interpreted as an expression of the vitality of Christian awareness of the faith and its utterances, there is certainly no historical justification for taking such an interpretation to be the 'real' meaning of Paul or of one of the other witnesses testifying to the primitive Christian proclamation of the resurrection. The point of the references to Jesus's resurrection is much better grasped if, as a large number of other commentators have done, one sums up the sense in the following sentence. Christ has risen in the kerygma (*proclamation*) (R. Bultmann). This formulation, which has become a slogan, was originally intended as an antithesis stated in an extreme form for the sake of clarity in order to underline the contrast with those (such as, for example, W. Künneth) who maintained that the sense of the resurrection was in the 'reality' of its having happened.

It is indeed appropriate to give prominence to the event of the proclamation, mission in its concrete historical widest sense, as the goal of the appearances of the risen Christ. However it is an anachronism to link with this the verdict that Jesus's resurrection as a separate event is of no theological concern since it is not concerned with anything other than the power of the proclamation of the crucified Christ, for this is a specific motif of 'Modern Theology', according to which the occurrence of salvation is concentrated in Christ's death on the Cross, which is here being transferred back into primitive Christianity. Certainly Christ's death 'for our sins' (1 Cor. 15:3) is of central significance, particularly in the theological thinking of Paul. But this sentence only derives its full strength from the conviction that God's creative power has raised the crucified Christ from the dead, and thereby demonstrated the effectiveness of his love. If the raising of Jesus from the dead were not an event valid in its own right, God's mighty deed carried out on the crucified Jesus, then the Pauline use of the expression 'the message of the Cross' would have had no force.

After all the effectiveness of the resurrection in the existence of the believers is measured by the fact that they become able and strong to do effective deeds of righteousness, and become capable and powerful in love (Romans 6:4–12ff; Gal. 5:6). Certainly they have to take upon themselves suffering, and certainly they have constantly to overcome their selfishness, but discipleship of Christ does not only consist in this! Not in letting myself be crucified with Christ or by giving up fame and refusing to push through my own will, do I succeed in living up to my faith in Christ in my own life, but by allowing myself to be provoked into doing deeds of love by the supreme sign of God's love revealed in his raising from the dead the crucified Christ. In the references in primitive Christianity to Jesus's resurrection what is decisive is that here God's creative omnipotence has become effective. Faith in Christ is, in primitive Christian terms, belief in the crucified Christ raised from the dead, and by inference consequently *belief in God in its greatest possible intensity*, namely belief in God who elevated his representative out of death to himself.

In what does Jesus represent God, however? In considering the basic thoughts of Paul, we already gave the answer in advance. According to Paul, (cf. p. 25f above), it is indeed the crucified Christ who in giving himself to *death* represents God, namely, the *love* of God. Love is, in its biblical sense, doing good for others. Love in this sense is made perfect, where a person gives his life for another person (Gal. 2:20; John 15:13) —more than this, where he does so for his foes (Rom. 5:6–8). By dying for those who are not righteous but wicked sinners, God's foes, Christ represents God's love towards them. However much belief in God's love depends on the proclamation of the *raising from the dead* of the crucified Christ by God's mighty deed, the essential point about this mighty deed is that it is the *crucified Christ* who was raised from the dead. This is the essential point because it means that it is love which brought God's mighty deed into effect.

The point about faith in the crucified Christ raised from the dead is that it is no other power than the power of love which finally comes to rule, and love which it is intended should hold sway. In this sense the *Cross* is the sign and symbol of what is Christian. Trust in the Cross, however, and the enormous drive and impetus which derive their power from the Cross, are ultimately based on the raising from the dead of the crucified Christ. If the meaning and direction of Christianity stand or fall with belief in the Cross of Christ, then the power of this belief stands or falls with belief in the resurrection of the crucified Christ.

(c)  *The Resurrection of Jesus as Divine Confirmation of his Effective Work*

We must take another and final step from here. We will again take up the question which remained unanswered at the end of the last chapter and try to answer it. How did belief in the resurrection arise? The result of our investigation hitherto was that, how belief in the resurrection arose, remains a historical riddle. Is that all? Is this as far as one can go? Now there is one circumstance we have not included in our explanation, and that is the decisive fact that it was *Jesus of Nazareth* who was recognized by the witnesses on his appearances, and it was Jesus of Nazareth whom they meant in their proclamation of the resurrection. Although they had recognized him as raised from the dead by God, this meant for them at the same time that God through this act had endorsed, with all the validity of his verdict at the end of time, the fact that Christ was right, and that God had recognized Christ as the Righteous One. In surrounding Judaism the resurrection was expected in connection with the Final Day of Judgment and the sense of it can only be understood in this framework.

The idea of the resurrection of a single individual in advance of the events at the end of time was not generally known in Judaism. One cannot assume therefore that the disciples of Jesus could of their own accord easily have attained the certainty that their Teacher had not remained in death, but had been raised from the dead, and argue that their visions could be explained as being only the expression of this certainty. Even if, in the context of the Jewish expectation of a return of the prophet Elijah at the end of time, there is found an isolated example of the idea that Elijah will then suffer the fate of all the prophets and die and rise again after three days, this idea could at the most be regarded as a possible aid to understanding what Jesus's disciples had experienced in his appearance, but is not to be regarded as a direct source of this experience. A riddle remains. We have here a cognition process which cannot be traced back to any pre-existing conditions. However once given the initial insight, as a result of the realization, brought about by the experience of Christ's appearances, that Jesus has been raised from the dead, then it was easy indeed for the other associated statements to be linked with it, namely, that he has been installed in heaven as Messiah, as Son of God, as Lord. He is the Righteous One, to whose sufferings testimony is borne in the Psalms, whom God has saved from death, the death caused by his foes, and of whose righteousness God has given eternal confirmation.

Having said all this we have still not specified the essence of the matter, namely, the answer to the question *who* this Jesus was. Who was this Jesus, who now appeared as the Risen One, the heavenly Mediator of Salvation, the Righteous One raised on high by God? In raising *him* from the dead, God had also by so doing, established that *his movement*, his preaching and teaching are right, and validated this in terms of his Final Judgment. For what Jesus, through his being raised from the dead, had now become, counted after all as valid confirmation of what Jesus *was*, as shown by what he did. The sense of all the sovereignty titles conferred on the risen Christ in primitive Christianity is derived originally from what Jesus previously *was*, in the record of his works. It would have been appropriate at this point to give a synopsis of the sayings and the doings of the 'historic Jesus'. However, we have only scope to indicate what is most important, in this volume. Readers are referred to the parallel volume by Herbert Braun in this series (*Jesus*, 'Themen der Theologie', Kreuz-Verlag, Stuttgart) and the volume by Günther Bornkamm, *Jesus of Nazareth* (translated by I. and F. McLuskey with J. M. Robinson, London, 1960).

The heart of Jesus's proclamation is his proclamation that the rule of God will become reality at the end of time both for the righteous and for sinners. 'From that day Jesus began to proclaim the message: "Repent; for the Kingdom of Heaven is upon you" ' (Matt. 4:17, NEB). This message is entirely in line with thinking in the history of the Jewish faith. The God whom Jesus proclaims is the God of Israel, who chose the Fathers and promised them justice and righteousness and demanded righteousness of them, the God who as Lord has creative almighty power and holds sway over the reality and the continuing existence of all things and all happenings and who has promised to employ his might for the salvation of his Chosen Ones. The Kingdom of God is nothing other than this, namely, the realization at the end of time for all eternity of the salvation of God's chosen ones and simultaneously the destruction of all foes and oppressors, all unrighteous and wicked sinners, consigned to eternal damnation; in other words, the execution of Final Judgment determining the eternal fate of men.

We have described above, (p. 80f), how Israel was affected increasingly deeply by the problem that God's justice and righteousness did not correspond to Israel's righteousness. From the time when the prophets confronted Israel with its sin and announced God's 'wrath' as a consequence of their doings the problem of the sin of the Chosen Ones was never given a rest. The best Israelites, to whom most credence was given, were those who insisted on application of the connection between sin and damnation, also, and most especially, to the Chosen People, and who on this account were most deeply disturbed about the final destiny of Israel. Although the experience of earlier history showed that God could take pity on sinners, overlook sins, forgive sins, and despite the fact that pious circles in particular entreated and implored God in their prayers to forgive the people fallen into sin, nevertheless it was correspondingly just as clear that the inflexible basic principle of God's Final Judgment must remain immutable, namely, that only those who have passed probation and justified their selection as Chosen Ones by their righteousness shall be granted eternal salvation and that all sinners by contrast shall be consigned to eternal damnation. John the Baptist renewed the preaching of the prophets with extreme increased intensity, calling on sinners to repent and carry out deeds of righteousness before it was too late—as it soon would be (Matt. 3:7–10).

The Baptist's call to repentance was taken up by Jesus. The atmosphere however has completely changed. The deep seriousness of the Baptist preaching penitence and repentance before the coming Judgment has given place to liberating jubilation. For, whereas the Baptist called the sinners to repent in view of the imminent Day of Judgment, Jesus's call to

repentence is against the background of the simple assurance of
salvation for all who now turn to God. God makes no difference
between the righteous and sinners in his Kingdom, which he is
now beginning to bring to completion, all are welcome. Indeed
the angels in heaven rejoice more over a single sinner who
repents 'than over ninety-nine righteous people who do not
need to repent' (Luke 15:7, NEB).

Therefore Jesus's call is addressed primarily to sinners, and
in telling provocation of the pious he joined the very people
who were publicly regarded in Israel as irrevocably lost sinners
and celebrated their acceptance into the Kingdom of Heaven
with joyful celebrations, eating and drinking with taxgatherers,
prostitutes and other notorious sinners (Mark 2:15; Matt.
11:19). For 'It is not the healthy that need a doctor, but the
sick; I did not come to invite virtuous people, but sinners'
(Mark 2:17, NEB). This naturally does not mean that Jesus in a
'transvaluation of all values' was rejecting the righteous and
had joined in solidarity with the sinners. Sin remains sin, and
the consequence of sin remains eternal damnation; and 'unless
you repent, you will all of you come to the same end' (Luke
13:5, NEB).

Conversely the righteous person of course has his place
in his father's house (Luke 15:31). But Jesus wants to win
round the righteous to accepting God's decision to accept
sinners and not to stand in the way of God's saving
action. If the righteous would not accept, as Jesus did,
sinners, who have been pardoned, as their brothers, then
the righteous would lose the righteousness they had hitherto so
long preserved, now so soon before the end; for, anyone aiming
to establish some permanent distinction of the righteous and
pious and in consequence set himself up as a righteous person
in the sight of God keeping his distance apart from sinners
(Luke 18:10–14) is not acting in the way God acts. If God has
brought into effect his righteousness in order to bring about the
salvation of sinners, then it follows that no one can be a
righteous person if he disputes this. That is the point of the

parable of the two brothers (Luke 15:11–32). The joyful welcome home accorded to the lost son by the father should be paralleled by a similar joyful reception by his brother. The righteous people who have all their lives been just and righteous, should not be upset when they receive the same eternal reward as those who have only repented at the very last. God's salvation does not have any class distinction (Matt. 20:1–16: Parable of the labourers in the vineyard).

Correspondingly, the decisive criterion of righteousness is the love of the lost brother revealed in the doings of the forgiven sinners. Therefore God's Final Judgment will equate a person who is angry with his brother, with a murderer (Matt. 5:21): and just as God makes his sun rise on good and bad alike and sends the rain on the honest and the dishonest, so too they ought, as righteous ones in God's Kingdom, to love their enemies (Matt. 5:43–45). Just as God has forgiven, so too people should forgive one another, without limits (Matt. 18:21ff; Luke 17:3f; Matt. 6:14f; Luke 11:5ff). And the judge at the Day of Judgment will measure people's *relationship to God* in terms of the good which people have done to *each other* (Matt. 25:31ff). It can thus be said that Jesus's preaching of the nearness of the Kingdom of God in its main concern is a sermon on love as the final decisive might. God is the advocate of love. Accordingly a person is only seen fully when viewed through the eyes of love and seen as the person he is intended to be; and only in doing deeds of love is there perfection (Matt. 5:48, cf. Luke 6:36!).

If the disciples now after Jesus's death through God's 'revelation' perceived this Jesus, the Preacher of the Kingdom of God, as the Risen One, ultimately vindicated by God at the end of time, then *what they saw in their risen Master, was, essentially, the eternal vindication of love as the final deciding might.* For Jesus himself was so essentially, so completely at one with his message that his own justification in heaven was simultaneously the justification of his proclamation. Just as the disciples got to see the risen Christ in the position and function he is to occupy at the end of time, so too the divine confirmation of his message, which this contained, was also God's final decision. The victory of love, whose coming to eternal power Jesus had proclaimed, is thus the final future which men are to expect. For God however this future is already decided; for, God has raised from the dead and taken up to himself Jesus, who had announced the beginning of the Kingdom and the reality of its proximity. Accordingly at the same time as they experienced Jesus's resurrection, the disciples also experienced the confirmation of their own discipleship to Jesus in the light of the end of time. For Jesus himself had promised those who confess their allegiance to him here and now on earth, that the heavenly Judge at the end of time will likewise take their side (Luke 12:8f).

The disciples now recognized that this Judge at the end of time, the 'Son of Man' was none other than their Master raised from the dead and arisen into heaven (cf. the post-Easter version of the Saying of Luke 12:8f in Matt. 10:32f). From here they deduced their right to regard their belonging to him as being the same as belonging to the Son of Man and that means, as being confirmed as being the same too as belonging to God and his Kingdom. The community of disciples of Jesus was henceforth the chosen community of salvation at the end of time, the 'Church of God'. Since then in Christianity relationship to *God* is determined essentially and continuously by the relationship to *Jesus*.

Finally, this also explains the fact that the appearances of the risen Christ were experienced by the witnesses essentially as their vocation to their task, their call to mission. Now they were to continue his proclamation on earth: and if first of all they turned this into reality, corresponding to Jesus's movement in Galilee, as a prophetic mission preaching to Israel (Matt. 10:5–7, 23) nevertheless the universal horizon and the end of time perspective implicit in Jesus's proclamation of the Kingdom of God soon led to the disciples going beyond he frontiers of Israel seeking to bring 'all nations' to be disciples of Jesus (Matt. 28:18f; Mark 13:10). Going on from this, Paul consciously and deliberately promoted World Mission and proclaimed the Gospel of Christ as the comprehensive deed of salvation of God's righteousness, for all, for heathens and Jews, as the justification of sinners (Rom. 1:16f). All of this, the history of mission in primitive Christianity and the entire history of Christian thought with its many layers, is to be understood as an effect of the original experience of the resurrection of Jesus, the preacher of love. If it were not for this experience Christianity would undoubtedly not have come into existence. Through this experience Christianity as a whole is given its basis.

Therefore it is one of the elementary tasks of Christian theology to strive for a proper understanding of the testimony to the resurrection in primitive Christianity. Even if today the whole structure of the Jewish apocalyptic way of thinking in which historically this testimony is embedded, strikes us as alien, and even if primitive Christianity's statement that Jesus arose from the dead runs counter to our understanding of reality, nevertheless that should be no reason for the person who is aware of his own most profound commitment to the Christian faith to disregard the question as to the original meaning and point of the testimony about the resurrection, or casually fit it into his own customary motives and usual way of thinking. Likewise there is no reason to regard the enquiry about Jesus's resurrection as senseless and antiquated, nor to regard the attempt to find convincing contemporary ways of envisaging the happening of the resurrection as a hopeless apologetical undertaking.

There is no reason for these prejudiced attitudes because, if we are to be entirely just and do justice to the 'heart of the matter' in the primitive Christian testimony about the resurrection, then we must take into account its dependence both on the Jewish thought context, and the fact, and manner, of proclamation of the raising from the dead of Jesus having taken place. The basic reason for all the religious and moral world-

changing elan which has hitherto characterized Christianity,
is that what the New Testament proclaims as God's deed in
Jesus is true. We cannot grasp the full truth of this—even as
understood by primitive Christianity—if our enquiry restricts
itself to determining in isolation what actually happened or
may have happened at the beginning. We are not doing justice
to the truth of the original testimony and the experiences
transmitted in the testimony if we only establish that what the
New Testament reports narrate as events, did 'historically'
actually take place; nor are we doing justice to the full truth
either if we demand that, contrary to all reasoning and
knowledge, we must just simply 'believe' that what was
impossible nevertheless 'really' happened through God's
almighty power.

The truth of the resurrection is revealed not in what was the
situation in the past but in what is contemporary: not in what
happened in the past, but in what is happening in the way of
continuing effects produced by its stimulus throughout history
and still occurring. All true Christian commitment has also
come from the truth of Jesus's resurrection. This truth is
already at work and effective in the Christian and his world,
even before he begins to try to understand it. Understanding of
truth even if it follows on after the existence and effective
action of the truth, is nevertheless indispensable and it must not
be short-circuited. The sort of understanding which is required
is not an anachronistic understanding of Christian truth in
terms of our contemporary apperception. What we have to do,
is to make the effort to retrace in detail and spell out what the
New Testament testimony is saying. Only such an understanding of the New Testament message will retain the
necessary power to give continually renewed stimulus to
Christian life.

# For Further Reading

Texts suitable for non-specialists are indicated by an asterisk.

*Texts other than New Testament texts*
*E. Kautzsch, *Die Apokryphen und Pseudepigraphen des Alten Testaments* (1921): or its equivalent:
R. H. Charles, *The Apocrypha and Pseudepigrapha of the Old Testament in English* (1913).
*E. Hennecke, *New Testament Apocrypha*. Edited by R. M. Wilson, 2 vols (1963, 1965). Volume I contains the Peter Gospel. (German original 1959.)
*S. Krauss, *Das Leben Jesu nach jüdischen Quellen* (1902).

*From the history of scholarship*
Thomas Woolston, *Sixth Discourse on the Miracles of our Saviour* (1729).
Peter Annet, *The resurrection of Jesus considered in answer to the Trial of the witnesses*. By a Moral Philosopher (1744).
G. E. Lessing, *Theologische Schriften* (edited by L. Zscharnack), III (1910). (See the 'Fragments of the Unnamed Wolfenbüttler': V. On the Resurrection Story; VI. Of the purpose of Jesus and his disciples.)
D. F. Strauss, *Das Leben Jesu*, II (1836); available in various English translations, including one by 'George Eliot' (Marian Evans, afterwards Cross); most recently as, *The New Life of Jesus*.
*A. Meyer, *Die Auferstehung Jesu* (1905).
M. Goguel, *La foi à la résurrection de Jésus dans le christianisme primitif* (1933).

*From present-day exegetical work*
K. Berger, *Die Auferstehung des Propheten und die Erhöhung des Menschensohnes: Traditions-geschichtliche Untersuchungen zur*

*Deutung des Geschickes Jesu in frühchristlichen Texten* (Studien zur Umwelt des Neuen Testaments, 13) (1976).

L. Brun, *Die Auferstehung Christi in der urchristlichen Uberlieferung* (1925).

R. Bultmann, *Theology of the New Testament* (1965). (German 6th edition, 1968; sections 7 and 33.)

*H. v. Campenhausen, *Der Ablauf der Osterereignisse und das leere Grab* (1966).

H. Grass, *Ostergeschehen und Osterberichte* (1962).

J. Kremer, *Das älteste Zeugnis von der Auferstehung Jesu* (Stuttgarter Bibelstudien, 17) (1967).

*W. Künneth, *The Theology of the Resurrection* (1965).

K. Lehmann, *Auferweckt am dritten Tage nach der Schrift* (Quaestiones di(s)putatae 38) (1968).

*E. Lohse, *Die Auferstehung Jesu Christi im Zeugnis des Lukasevangeliums* (Biblische Studien 31).

W. Marxsen, U. Wilckens, G. Delling and H. G. Geyer, *The Significance of the Message of the Resurrection for Faith in Jesus Christ.* Edited by C. F. D. Moule (1968). (German original 1968.)

*W. Marxsen, *The Resurrection of Jesus of Nazareth* (1970). (German original 1968.)

W. Pannenberg, *Grundzüge der Christologie* (1966).

*K. H. Rengstorf, *Die Auferstehung Jesu* (Form, Art und Sinn der urchristlichen Osterbotschaft) (1960).

L. Schenke, *Auferstehungsverkündigung und leeres Grab* (Stuttgarter Bibelstudien, 33) (1968).

*Theologische Quartalschrift* 153 (1973): *Die Entstehung des Osterglaubens* (R. Pesch, *et al.*)